Market value

Its measurement and metric

Edward Fullbrook

World Economics Association Books

World Economics Association BOOK SERIES

Market-value: Its measurement and metric

by Edward Fullbrook

ISBN: 978-1-911156-41-3 (paperback)
978-1-911156-40-6 (eBook, Mobi)
978-1-911156-42-0 (eBook, PDF)

Published by World Economics Association, Bristol, UK
www.worldeconomicsassociation.org

The **World Economics Association (WEA)** was launched on May 16, 2011. Already over 13,000 economists and related scholars have joined. This phenomenal success has come about because the WEA fills a huge gap in the international community of economists – the absence of a professional organization which is truly international and pluralist.

The World Economics Association seeks to increase the relevance, breadth and depth of economic thought. Its key qualities are worldwide membership and governance, and inclusiveness with respect to: (a) the variety of theoretical perspectives; (b) the range of human activities and issues which fall within the broad domain of economics; and (c) the study of the world's diverse economies.

The Association's activities centre on the development, promotion and diffusion of economic research and knowledge and on illuminating their social character.

The WEA publishes books, three open-access journals (*Economic Thought, World Social and Economic Review* and *Real-World Economics Review*), a bi-monthly newsletter, blogs, holds global online conferences, runs a textbook commentaries project and an eBook library.

... the history of every science, including that of economics, teaches us that the elementary is the hotbed of the errors that count most.

— GEORGESCU-ROEGEN
American Economic Review 1970 (60-2) p. 9.

The difficulty lies, not in the new ideas, but in escaping from the old ones, which ramify, for those brought up as most of us have been, into every corner of our minds.

— JOHN MAYNARD KEYNES
The General theory of Employment, Interest and Money, 1936

Market-value is a human invention.

Acknowledgement

This book has significantly benefited from the comments of Jamie Morgan. The usual disclaimers pertain.

Contents

Warning

Given recent tradition in economics, it is likely that most readers will fundamentally misunderstand this book from cover to cover. Why? Because it is likely that they will think that its math (elementary abstract algebra) refers in some way to a model or models. But it doesn't.

There are two ways of using mathematics relative to an empirical phenomenon. One is to choose a mathematical structure and then make assumptions about the empirical structure so as to "make" the two structures homomorphic. This, the bread-and-butter methodology of today's economics orthodoxy, generates mathematical models from which concepts can be defined and deductions made. The other way is what Newton called "experimental philosophy". Instead of beginning with a mathematical structure, it *begins* by observing and describing an empirical structure and then looks for or invents (e.g. Newton's calculus) a homomorphic mathematical structure. It is then on this empirical foundation, rather than the axioms of a mathematics, that concepts are defined and deductions made.

This book seeks to identify and describe the metrical properties of the quantitative order of market-value *as it exists out there in the real-world.* In so doing it discovers that those elementary properties are radically different from what some of our best known theories and models *assume* them to be. You may, therefore, wish *not* to know what market-value's metric is. If so, read no further.

The plot

This book's plot structure is simple but foreign to economics and, therefore, easily missed. So here is the plot's outline.

1. Market-value, a general quantitative order, is what distinguishes economics from other social sciences.

2. A quantitative order has a metrical structure, called its metric.

3. Metrics vary between quantitative orders, e.g. length, temperature and angle.

4. Metrics are discovered by inventing and executing measurement operations on the quantitative orders.

5. The measurement of market-value differs from that of other quantitative orders in that both the invention and execution of its measurement operation, i.e. market exchange, predate and exist independently of scientific inquiry.

6. This independence enabled economics to unconsciously **assume** market-value's metric rather than **empirically identify** it.

7. This book breaks with that tradition by applying abstract algebra to market-value measurements so as to identify, rather than assume, market-value's metric.

8. This metric turns out to be radically different from the one unconsciously assumed in constructing economic theory.

9. With the real metric in view, large long-standing paradoxes in economics are immediately resolved.

10. Knowledge of market-value's metric also immediately reveals a universal macro→micro causal link that effects market-value measurements in all markets.

11. Analysis of the revealed metric shows how the macro→micro and micro→macro links are interconnected.

12. The macro→micro causal link can be manipulated through individual markets.

13. This link's openness to manipulation means that economics needs to include political economy.

14. Discovery of market-value's metric provides an empirically-based theoretical core that can embrace most heterodox economics and large parts of the neoclassical mainstream.

15. Public knowledge of market-value's metric is contrary to the interests of The One Percent.

Chapter 1

This book's central thesis

What distinguishes economics from all other social sciences is that it is based on a ubiquitous real-world quantitative order, market-value, which qualifies as a **measurement** order in the sense of the quantitative orders of physics. Market-value, including the never discussed assumption that it has the same formal structure as length and mass have at the micro or pre-Einsteinian level, is **the** most fundamental concept in economics. It is the existence of this measurement order together with the presumption regarding its structure that, beginning nearly two centuries ago, has enabled economics to develop a theoretical core which in its formal rigour and its purported explanatory reach is unparalleled in the social sciences. The edifice that stands on this theoretical core is sometimes labelled "neoclassical economics", sometimes "mainstream economics", but in this opening chapter will be labelled "EE", the first E signifying "equilibrium". For a century and a half, the world's intellectual thinking about economic reality has in the main been founded on EE.

EE proceeds on the basis of certain formal properties which it assumes characterize market-value as a quantitative order. EE's theoretical strength lies in this abstract inner core which enables it to be used to formulate a diverse and expanding range of applications. In general, the more abstract a system of thought – mathematics and formal logic being the most – the more widely can that system be applied. It is the abstract theoretical core of EE that both enables its dominance and makes it so difficult, despite its notorious falseness when applied to the real-world, to dethrone and replace with empirically based systems of thought and analysis.

Because EE's theoretical core appears to be so removed from concrete realities, it has been natural for its non-believers to concentrate their efforts on showing EE's failures at predicting and explaining particular categories of real-world economic events and showing how alternative theories are more successful. In some cases, the proponents of alternative theories have succeeded in winning acknowledgement of their theory's superiority with regard to a particular real-world category of events. By far the most outstanding example of such circumscribed worldly success is Keynes' *The General Theory*. But because the alternative theories lack the same degree of broad structural abstractness at their core – in many cases having almost none – their ideas either remain conceptually isolated from each other and from the economics discipline as a whole, or, as in the case of Keynes, are gradually emasculated so as to enable their co-optation under EE's theoretical core [Akerlof, 2001].

At first sight there appears to be no way to undermine EE's all-embracing conceptual stranglehold, the ultimate means by which EE maintains its hegemony on the economics discipline and thereby also on intellectual thought processes that govern societies. Because the structural core of EE is so abstract, it in and of itself has been regarded as immune from the possibility of *direct empirical falsification*. There have, of course, been innumerable applications of the theory that have shown it to be false, but invariably these have been interpreted as merely special cases. Also, various logical inconsistencies within the theory itself have been identified, mostly notably Sonnenschein [1972, 1973], Mantel [1974] and Debreu [1974], but also Shackle [1949], Sraffa [1960] and most recently Keen and Standish [2010]. But all these internal contradiction discoveries are effortlessly ignored. *The dual absence of a direct primary empirical falsification* (e.g., Galileo and his telescope, or the 1919 solar eclipse) *of EE's theoretical core and of an alternative all-encompassing abstract structure has rendered EE's hegemony invincible.*

The central thesis of this book, however, is that the dissenters from economics' tradition of *apriorism* have been too modest in their empiricism. It is conceivable that *there exists in real-world economies a universal structure*, an invisible foot, whose abstract properties are logically inconsistent with EE's *a priori* determined structure. If such a structure were to exist and to become known, then not only would EE's theoretical core be *empirically falsified*, but also most of the existing non-EE theories would then have *a common theoretical frame of reference*, and thereby the theoretical unity by which the long and increasingly destructive reign of EE could be terminated.

****

This book is based on two insights that came to me long ago when, following a period of studying the epistemology of physics through the centuries, I returned after an extended absence to economics. The book's cover image refers to one of those insights, but it is the other that came first and that is really the more fundamental. In reviewing the discipline from the distance gained by my absence and my recent interest, the *larger* structures of economics were visible to me in a way they never had been before.

One of those structures was the *hypothesis* – never stated except sometimes formally when defining mathematical models – that economics' only indigenous order of measurement, market-value (or "exchange-value" if you prefer) has the same algebraic structure as pre-Einsteinian mass and length. All of marginalism in so far as it pertains to market exchange depends upon this hypothesis. Two forgotten works by famous 20th century economists [Becker, 1962 and Patinkin, 1965] and an independent observation of my own suggested anomalies in this presumption and thus the possibility that **the market-value metric** might be radically different than what we economists – myself included – presumed every day of our working lives.

I searched the history of economics to find out how the hypothesis that market-value has this metric came to be and found NOTHING; no one appeared to have ever overtly made a case for it. Instead our belief in it – and again I include myself – came about in two ways. One is because at the everyday commercial level where we function as real-life individuals, market-value appears to be an additive quantity, in the same way that at the level of daily life the Sun appears to orbit the Earth. The other stems from the traditional way that economics uses mathematics. Whereas from Galileo on, physics looks for or invents mathematics that have the same structures that they are finding in the physical world[1], economics from Walras on tends to begin with the mathematics and then make assumptions about the economic world that will make it appear consistent with the mathematics they have chosen [Akerlof, 2001, p. 388].[2]

When you read Walras's *Elements of Pure Economics*, for example, this methodology is very much out in the open. This upside-down use of math in economics "works" because, unlike in physics, there are virtually no empirical checks and certainly no tradition of trying to make them. In the natural sciences if the wrong mathematics is chosen, the error will in time become manifest through empirical observation and acknowledged because of the scientists' commitment to empiricism, with the result that the theoretical process will be re-begun. But with EE the fundamental theoretical structures, most stemming from Walras and thereabouts, are only ever allowed to be questioned – and then usually only on the outer fringes of the faithful – in the immediate aftermath of a major economic crisis.

The exploration that underlies the second and third chapters of this book predates my interest and involvement in the pluralist and real-world movements in economics. It also was independent of any career or reputational ambitions, as – and for our time this is a confession of

---

[1] Or in Newton's words: "In this experimental philosophy, propositions are deduced from *the phenomena* and are made general by induction" [emphasis added] *The Principia: Mathematical Principles of Natural Philosophy*, University of California Press, Oakland, California, 1999, p. 589.

[2] For example, as Akerlof 2001, p. 388 describes: "Immediately after its [*The General Theory*] publication, the economics profession tamed Keynesian economics. They domesticated it as they translated it into the 'smooth' mathematics of classical economics."

sorts – I am capable of becoming for its own sake hedonistically absorbed over extended periods of time in the pursuit of comprehension of something for which my understanding is less than I would like. So in this case, having achieved the desired understanding, its publication, although sought and in part achieved [Fullbrook, 1992; 1993; 1994(b); 1996(a); 2002], was not for my inner self of great importance. New intellectual infatuations took hold and this earlier one was largely forgotten.

But *today* – even ignoring the economy-caused ecological crisis – *as economists we live in a fundamentally different historical situation.* The 40-year upwards redistribution of income and wealth, the accelerating growth of neo-fascism, the Global Financial Crisis, the mass reading of Piketty's *Capital in the Twenty-First Century* and, not least, the work in recent decades of many innovative economists – too many to list but well-represented in the *Real-World Economic Review* – have revealed a large real-life economic and political significance of my earlier empirically based analysis of economics' **inner-most theoretical core.**

****

Given the strong tradition of pseudoscience in economics, it seems likely that some readers will *completely* misunderstand Chapter 3. Although it contains quite a bit of elementary mathematics, it is in no way concerned with axiomatic deduction or models. Instead it contains mathematical expressions that are *direct empirical assertions* – none of them contentious – about the structure of market-value wherever and whenever it exists in the real-world, and are therefore either true or false, just as the assertion "The Earth orbits the Sun" is either true or false.

How can this be possible? It is possible because real-world *quantitative orders*, for example length and mass, have structures – and market-value is not a magical exception – whose characteristics can be *observed and described* with elementary abstract algebra, *thereby identifying an algebraic structure which is homomorphic to the empirical structure*. And it turns out that that structure is radically different from the one that for a century-and-a-half we economists have in our theorizing presumed it to be. Then, just as EE makes its theoretical deductions based on its *presumed* metric, this book will make a few elementary deductions based on market-value's *real* metric.

****

There are ***two key terms*** *in this book*, and they are defined as follows. "*Absolute quantitative order*" means a quantitative order whose instances, including their magnitudes, exist independently of other instances of that quantitative order. A "relative quantitative order" is one for which this condition does not hold. Length and mass in a Newtonian domain are examples of absolute quantities, and probability is an example of a relative quantitative order.

****

There are two primary dimensions to *the historical context of this book.*

The first is Keynes and his demonstration that the level of employment in an economy is not fully explicable by economics' traditional micro-reductionism. The parallel in physics is Maxwell's 1860s introduction of field theory which enabled heterodox physicists to begin thinking beyond the confines of its tradition of micro-reductionism.

Given economics' ideological and remunerative undercurrents, Keynes' break with micro-reductionism was an even more fundamental break with economics' status quo than was Maxwell's for physics and, therefore, was and is much more resisted. But 80 years have now passed and the focus of positive attention on Keynes' *The General Theory* has remained almost exclusively on the topic to which he applied his macro vision rather than on that vision itself, in particular its implications for keystone concepts of our discipline and, most important of all, discovering the missing **general macro→micro causal link** that it implies. It is the failure to do the last – to identify **the macro-foundations of micro-economics** – that has left macro-economics so vulnerable to co-optation by micro-reductionism.[3]

Like Maxwell, the primary genius of Keynes was his ability to think outside the then most elementary concepts of his discipline. But when a theorist ventures beyond her accustomed neighborhood she immediately encounters enormous problems because the routes and landmarks of her mental map no longer quite – and maybe hardly at all – lineup with her new position. There is a description of Keynes' *The General Theory* by Paul Samuelson, which is ironic given Samuelson's well-known disinclination to engage with the book's fundamentals, that aptly describes the kind of difficulties that theoretical scientists encounter when their empirical observations take then outside the scope of their science's most elementary conceptions.

---

[3] My "foundations" corresponds to "underlying structures and forces" when Lars Syll writes "the main task of science is... to identify and explain the underlying structure and forces that produce the observed events." https://larspsyll.wordpress.com/2018/12/21/inference-to-the-best-explanation-3/

> It abounds in mares' nests or confusions. In it the Keynesian system stands out indistinctly, as if the author were hardly aware of its existence or cognizant of its properties; and certainly he is at his worst when expounding its relations to its predecessors. Flashes of insight and intuition intersperse tedious algebra. An awkward definition suddenly gives way to an unforgettable cadenza. When finally mastered, its analysis is found to be obvious and at the same time new. In short, it is a work of genius [Samuelson 2014, pp. 400-401].

Two landmarks of the standard conceptual map that Keynes was still reliant upon were *equilibrium* and *market-value conceived as an absolute quantitative order*, neither of which aligned with his macro vision of employment determination and which together account for most of the "mares' nests" noted by Samuelson. This book's analysis is centered on those two fundamental difficulties that emerge when one begins to speculate that economic reality, like physical reality, has an *irreducible* macro dimension. It is this analysis that reveals the missing *macro→micro link.*

In terms of the longer history of the economics discipline, this book is *a synthesis of the theory of market-value and the theory of distribution*, or – with the insight that follows that integration – the demonstration that market-value and distribution of income and wealth are ultimately the same thing. As will be shown, their identity has heretofore escaped observation because *the metrical structure of market-value* has remained unknown, and apparently for no reason except that no one thought to ask, rather than to assume, what it is.

The long-term implications for economics of this discovery are enormous, as they radically and irreversibly undermine the traditional economics whose analytical apparatus is founded on the assumption that market-value's metric is radically different from what it is in fact. It also means, as will become clear in the pages that follow, that many dimensions of economic reality traditionally assumed to be purely economically determinate are in fact wide-open to psychological, social, cultural, political and speculator determination. Add to that the economy's now dire threat to the Earth's life-support system and economics is suddenly facing a long phase of future development fundamentally different from its past two centuries.

Chapter 2

Two gestalts: equilibrium and measurement

1. Introduction

The visual curiosity that adorns this book's cover first appeared in 1892 in a German humorous weekly but soon gained intellectual respectability through use in psychology textbooks, philosophy essays and, perhaps most famously, Gombrich's *Art and Illusion* [1977, p. 4] "Rabbit or Duck?" belongs to a genre of pictures readable in two radically different ways and whose presentation normally includes an indication of their two-sidedness. Without help, viewers usually see only one of the images, the one which their past most predisposes them to see. This chapter will argue that, like the famous drawing, there are two ways to see economic analysis, but that one has never been seen very clearly and in the last century hardly at all.

2. Equilibrium Economics (EE)

Before revealing this book's rabbit, we need to examine its metaphorical duck, *equilibrium economics*. This method of analysis interprets the economy as a system of markets tending toward equilibrium. On its own, the equilibrium concept is an empirically neutral one, used by many theoretical sciences. The following definition, taken from a thermodynamics textbook, illustrates the equilibrium concept in its abstract form:

> A system is in a state of equilibrium if no finite rate of change of its state can occur without some corresponding finite change of state, either temporary or permanent, in its environment [Montgomery, 1966, p. 7].[1]

As with any abstract concept, the key terms of the equilibrium notion require empirical interpretation before a given science can put it to use. The "system" must be identified in terms of a finite set of variables; the "state" in terms of a subset of the system set, and then methods of count, measurement, and computation must be established for describing the rates of change in the state variables.

However, empirical interpretation rarely suffices to make the equilibrium concept a useful one. Usually it is also necessary to conjecture a hypothesis *vis-a-vis* the interpreted equilibrium concept, namely, that *the system in some way tends toward equilibrium*. This has been the case for equilibrium economics, whose analytical engine is the implicit but sweeping *empirical* hypothesis that the *market system tends toward equilibrium*, with "prices and quantities" being taken as the state variables.

In individual markets when there are changes in supply and/or demand, price adjustments are made that within

[1] Since "equilibrium" comes from the Latin meaning "equal weight", an even more neutral way of stating the concept would be to substitute the words "terminating state" for the words "state of equilibrium".

that market lead toward a *static* situation. Everyone, not just economists, tends to observe these equilibrating tendencies. And against the broad background of these everyday observations, it is counterintuitive *not* to presume that this inherent tendency to move toward a static situation at the micro level is not generally at work for the economy as a whole. However, as we will see, the real-world possibility of reaching a macro or general market-based equilibrium depends on the metrical structure of market-value.

Viewing markets as **equilibrium systems** lends itself to the construction of a formal system of analysis, wherein the equilibrium state acts as the point of reference or solution principle for the theorist. The theoretical focus becomes identification of equilibrium values for the state variables, price and quantity. This pursuit includes a challenging set of analytical problems:

- Equilibrium's existence,
- necessary and sufficient conditions for equilibrium,
- stability and uniqueness of equilibrium situations, and
- adjustment paths between equilibria.

3. The duck's bill is the rabbit's ears

Central to equilibrium analysis is the process of price determination. Tradition views it as the principal adjustment mechanism by which markets move from disequilibrium states to equilibrium ones. From this vantage-point, price appears as *a "control" variable* which adjusts quantity demanded to quantity supplied. In this kind of analysis, price determination serves as the principal *means* by which economics explains the realization of equilibrium states. Or, in technical terms, price determination functions as the explanans for equilibrium, the explanandum phenomenon. These epistemological roles of price determination and equilibrium, however, can be reversed. But what would be gained by such a reversal and how would it proceed?

One finds a clue in price theory's alternative name, the theory of value. Economic literature uses the word "price" to denote not just one quantitative order, but several, including:

- units of money,
- units of money per unit of some commodity,
- units of market-value and
- units of market-value per unit of some commodity.

The possibility of using the same term for designating a quantity of tokens and for designating a quantity of a property of those tokens exists because the tokens are used to define a unit of the latter, that is, market-value. The term "value" or "market-value" not only avoids the ambiguity of the term "price"; it also begins to bring into focus *the attribute of economic reality most congenial to scientific methodology.* A quantity of market-value, instead of referring to a quantity of things, as do quantities of money and quantities of commodities, refers to a *property* which is a characteristic of a wide class of things, in this case money and the sets of all assets and commodities. Furthermore, market-value is not merely a putative or make-believe quantitative property, such as utility. Rather it is one, like the physical properties of mass, length and time, for which numbers are assigned to objects on a regular and systematic basis. The assignment of such numbers, that is, those which describe a property, rather than being merely numbers of count, are *numbers of measurement*. This distinction between quantities of things and quantities of properties has, of course, been fundamental to the development of post-Aristotelian science. All physical objects have mass and extension and all economic objects have, or potentially have, market-value. The theoretical edifices of modern science, including equilibrium economics, have been constructed on the basis of this universality of the *measurement mode of numerical description*.

The **measurement process** we call "price determination" underwrites our understanding of a market economy. As a measurement order, however, there is something truly unique about market-value: ITS MEASUREMENT IS *INTERNAL* TO THE OBJECT OF INQUIRY.[2] (What is meant by this will become clearer in Chapter 3.) Economists do not assign market-value *numbers* to commodities. Instead, the very people whose behaviour economics studies also generate these *measurement numbers*. This internality of the market-value *measurement relation*, to my knowledge, is without parallel in the scientific world. Yet, so far as I know, the first person to comment on it was Wassily Leontief. In 1983 he wrote as follows.

> "As an empirical science, economics dealt from the outset with phenomena of common experience.... Even the application of the scientific principle of quantification did not have to be initiated by the analyst himself – measuring and pricing constitute an integral

[2] This process of market-value measurement will be closely examined in Chapter 3.

> part of the phenomena that he sets out to explain. Herein lies, however, the initial source of the trouble in which academic economics finds itself today" [Leontief, 1983, pp. vii-viii].

Generations of analysts have failed to comprehend or explain this *fundamental dimension of economic reality*. Surely this is because, when *viewing the economy through the equilibrium analogy*, the pricing process is not seen primarily, if at all, as a measurement one. With one's mind under the sway of the equilibrium gestalt, all the various aspects of the market process are assigned meaning and significance in ways which fill in the equilibrium "picture". Similarly, when the Rabbit or Duck drawing is viewed under the spell of the duck gestalt, the scissors-like protrusions are interpreted as a bill. It is only when one goes looking for a rabbit, that the bill is transformed into a pair of ears. Will similar transformations take place if we follow Leontief's suggestion, change economics' gestalt, and interpret the market in the first instance not as a process of reaching equilibrium but rather *as a process of measurement*?

4. Measurement economics (ME)

Viewing an empirical phenomenon from a *measurement* perspective means asking questions such as the following.

- What is the property being measured?
- What are the mathematical characteristics of the scale on which it is expressed?
- Is the mode of comparing concrete magnitudes of the property direct or indirect?

- What is the operation of measurement?
- What is its equivalence relation?
- What objects are used as the standards of measurement?
- What are the procedures by which those standards are specified?
- Is the measured property an absolute one like mass or a relative one like motion?
- If the property is relative, what is it relative to?
- What is the process by which the measurement standard is used to define a measurement unit?
- What is the combining operation for the standards and for the objects to be measured?
- Is the property additive, and, if so, under what empirical operation?
- Does the measurement order have any special characteristics, for example, like the upper bound of velocity?
- Are there any micro-macro or extreme magnitude problems, such as the scale and equivalence relation breakdowns which Einstein revealed for physical quantities?
- And, most important, **what exactly is the quantitative property's metric?**

Please note that none of these questions are about models. Once their abstract terms are given empirical meanings, *they are all strictly empirical questions.* Market-values and their measurement numbers, as with mass, length and time, are real-world, everyday and nearly everywhere phenomena; and it is to their real-world, i.e. empirical existence, that these questions will be directed. How is this possible? It is possible in the same way that it is possible for physical quantities. Just as one can inquire (and as physicists have done for centuries) as to the basic structural properties of mass, length and time and of the scales of their measurement numbers, we should be able to do and will do the same for market-value. We will also see in this chapter and in Chapter 3 that in the past some prominent economists have tried to answer some of these questions.

Empirically interpreting the above 15 analytical questions in terms of markets and market-value creates a research agenda. For some questions, the answers come easily.

- In a money economy, measured quantities of market-value are expressed, like length, mass and time, on a ratio scale.
- Market exchanges generate these measurement numbers and therefore beg to be studied as measurement operations.
- In these operations, quantities of money serve as replicated measurement standards exchanged for quantities of a commodity,
- And equilibrium, *now part of the explanans*, serves as the equivalence relation.

This way of looking at market phenomenon leads the observer scientist to see the market's equilibrium quantity of money as a number of equivalent measurement standards which, because of the satisfaction of the empirical equivalence relation of market equilibrium, assigns a measurement number to the quantity of the good exchanged. Thus, this simple but profound change in preconceptions opens a radically different perceptual world. Where before there were equilibrium and equilibrium quantities (and still are merely by filtering our observations through the equilibrium perspective), now there are measurement standards, an operationally defined equivalence relation, measurement numbers and the possibilities of accuracy and inaccuracy.

If the quantitative property of market-value is not an absolute one, then: *to **what** is the market-value of an object relative?* This question and those which follow it in the above list are not easily answered for markets and market-value. These scientifically challenging queries, with their profound implications for economics as a whole, divide into two fields of enquiry.

5. Two fields of measurement analysis

a. The relativity problem

The proposed difference in the content of *measurement analysis* and *equilibrium analysis* corresponds to a remarkable degree to the division existing in physics since the 14th century, namely that between kinematics and dynamics. The latter seeks to discover the causes of motion, whereas the former is the science of pure motion, considered without reference to mass or force or collision. Kinematics, the more fundamental of the two branches, seeks to establish the basic properties or structure of the phenomenon, whose causes dynamics then aims to discover. Kinematics' dedication to *first-order questions*, made it the inevitable source of both the major revolutions in physics since Aristotle.

Realization of motion's relative nature came only by stages at long historical intervals. Awareness that motion, unlike mass and extension, is a relative phenomenon underlined the need for a science dealing exclusively with the *description of motion's abstract properties*. As Galileo and Einstein [Einstein, 1952] showed, relativity, even when it involves simple physical objects – like moving trains and falling stones – is not a relation with which even the finest human intellect is naturally at ease. So simple scientific prudence demanded discovery and description of the *properties* of motion before attempting to discover its *causes*.

A similar prudence has not prevailed in economics. Not only is market-value a **relative** quantitative order, as will be rigorously shown in Chapter 3, but it has taken human understanding even longer to grasp fully this capital fact than it did the relativity of motion. Merely a century and a half ago the prevailing wisdom among economists was that market-value was absolute in nature, a belief that persists to the present day in some quarters. This "absolutist" doctrine characterized not only Ricardo's labour theory of value, wherein market-value was reducible to quantities of labour, but also Condillac and Say's theory which asserted that market-value was reducible to quantities of utility. Only toward the middle of the 19th century did formal realization of market-value's relativity begin. This process was so gradual, however – and eventually closed down – that it is very much open to argument as to who was the primary source. A case can be made for Cournot; an even better one for the little-known Samuel Bailey, who in 1825 argued that market-value is, like motion, an irreducibly relative phenomenon. Subsequently this hypothesis that market-value, whatever its causes, was a **relation** between things was taken up and expounded by Bastiat and Cournot in France, A. L. Perry in America, Cairnes in Ireland, Cherbuliez in Switzerland, and John Stuart Mill in England.

The relativity hypothesis led immediately to two new questions that fall within the domain of *measurement economics:* **How many terms are there in the market-value relation and what are they?**

Economists struggled to answer these measurement questions in the half century following the publication of Bailey's *A Critical Dissertation on the Nature, Measure and Causes of Value*. Mill, in his *Principles* of 1848, summed up the emerging wisdom, before going on to describe one enormous unsolved problem.

> ...the value of a commodity is not a name for an inherent and substantive quality of a thing itself, but means the quantity of other things which can be obtained in exchange for it. The value of one thing must always be understood relatively to some other thing or to things in general [1848, Book III, Ch. 3, Sec. 1].

Mill's words "relatively to some other thing or to things in general", summarise the central dilemma that faced the pioneers of modern economics. Is market-value a relation *between two goods* or a relation *between a good and goods in general*? Both ideas seem essential: on the one hand exchange takes place between pairs of things, and on the other the existence of money suggests that market-value is simultaneously a relation between all goods. But by the law of identity, market-value can not be both of these relations unless one can be shown to be reducible to the other. The endeavour **to discover the market-value relation** threw up a further obstacle, one that for a long time seemed insurmountable: How in this context could the words "goods in general" be given a scientific meaning? Mill described the impasse as follows:

> ...we shall henceforth understand . . . by the value, or exchange-value of a thing, its general power of purchasing; the command which its possession gives over purchasable commodities in general. What is meant by command over commodities in general? The same thing exchanges for a great quantity of some commodities, and for a very small quantity of others [Mill, 1848, Book III, Ch. 1, Sec. 1].

Mill concluded that it was "impossible to say" what was meant by "command over commodities in general", thereby belying his often quoted remark that nothing remained to be cleared-up concerning the theory of value [ibid.] By resisting the temptation to gloss over this central question, i.e., establishing rules of correspondence for economics' only indigenous order of measurement, Mill rose above the epistemological complacency of a discipline not subject to the rigours of empirical falsification. And although Mill lacked the tools to advance the identification of the market-value relation, his forthright critique of the problems provided a valuable legacy.

Walras took up that inheritance a quarter of a century later, bringing a much more formidable kit of mathematical reasoning to bear on *economics' most fundamental theoretical problem*. Walras also (arguably more than anyone before or since) perceived both the rabbit and the duck of economics. His *Elements* frequently treats, sometimes overtly, market exchange as a measurement operation [Walras, 1954].

Moreover, although Walras lacked a formal concept of an equivalence relation, this is one of the interpretations he gives to the market equilibrium relation. His treatment of the value question also seems influenced by his knowledge of physics. Indeed, there exists strong circumstantial evidence that Walras not only studied Newton's *Principia*, but that he used it as a formal model for his own heroic effort. An eccentricity of Newton's *Principia* is that its first two books are written without reference to units of measurement. Instead quantities of the same order are expressed as standing in certain ratios to each other [Menger, 1959]. Walras adopted a similar approach toward quantities of market-value. He also understood the need to demonstrate that market-value really is a magnitude and to identify its mathematical properties, before looking for its causes [Walras, 1954, pp. 70-1]. But beyond repeatedly illustrating, often through analogies with physical measurement, that market-value is a relative phenomenon, Walras never isolated *its formal structure*. Instead, although I doubt that it was his intention, his interpretation of the numeraire commodity resulted in the opposite. He posited the numeraire commodity as having "market-value" with radically different metrical properties from the "market-value" of all the other commodities. The numeraire commodity has, although never explicitly stated, unitary elasticity across all levels of exchange, in other words, a "market-value" that like Newton's mass and length is an additive absolute quantity. Without this additivity the commodity would be useless as a numeraire. These issues will be examined formally and closely in Chapter 3.

Regarding market-value's status as a quantitative order, however, the whole of Walras' argument culminating in his Theorem of General Equilibrium can be interpreted as an attempt to demonstrate that market-value really does, i.e., in a scientific sense, *qualify as a magnitude*. In fact, this most famous of theorems offers an encounter between equilibrium and measurement economics at their most fundamental levels. To explain how this is so it is necessary first to return to Mill.

The Ricardian tradition of focusing on the difficulty of comparing market-values over time defeated Mill's attempt to identify market-value as a quantitative order whose domain was goods in general. Although Mill, like Walras, lacked the formal concepts of connectivity and transitivity, his analysis was guided by intuition of these properties, including their importance to the question of market-value. He sensed the apparently impossible challenge which the passage of time posed for the satisfaction of these formal properties *vis-a-vis* market-value. The following excerpt shows the source of Mill's defeatism.

> The value of a thing in exchange for some commodities may be rising, for others falling. A coat may exchange for less bread this year than last... but for more glass or iron... Has the value of the coat, under these circumstances, fallen or risen? It is impossible to say: all that can be said is, that it has fallen in relation to one thing, and risen in respect to another [Mill, 1848, Book III, Ch. 1, Sec. 1].

Walras realized that it was premature to introduce time into the analysis of market-value. This was the foundation for his "success". From the beginning, he limited his analysis of market-value to a single point in time. By so doing he avoided the difficulties which had overwhelmed Mill. Walras explains his new and more circumscribed methodology as follows:

> Certainly, all values are in a continual process of change, as we well know. This only means that we cannot make any comparisons between values from place to place or from time to time, but that does not preclude us from comparing them with one another and measuring them at a given place and at *a given moment*. These are the conditions [we are told] under which we *measure* values [Walras, 1954, p. 187, emphasis added].

To his eternal credit, however, Walras did not merely presume the logical possibility of comparing market-values with one another "at a given place and at a given moment". Instead he sought to show how from the concept of relative market-value, that is "the value of one thing... relatively to some other thing" [Mill, 1848], a composite relation could be formulated which gave scientific meaning to the notion of market-value relative "to commodities in general". This required identifying the market conditions under which exchange operations would result in a quasi-serial or linear ordering of the universal commodity set. Such an arrangement would formally establish market-value as a quantitative relation whose domain was the aggregate endowment, i.e., "commodities in general", and not just a comparative relation between two commodities. For this ordering to exist, all commodities had to be connected by the relation of exchange and all triads of exchange ratios had to be transitive. Today the concept of a quasi-serial ordering, with its constituent notions of equivalence and precedence relations, symmetry, connectivity and transitivity is widely known. Walras, however, was attempting to identify the market-value relation before the invention of either abstract algebra or of the algebra of relations.

Usually once an equivalence relation has been operationally interpreted, only the transitivity condition remains empirically contingent for the establishment of a quantitative, i.e., quasi-serial or linear, order. Walras, without the benefit of today's formally developed mathematical ideas, understood this with amazing clarity as regards market-value. His insight on this crucial matter is salient in his celebrated Lesson 11 [Section lll], where he undertook to solve what is *the central problem not only for equilibrium economics but also for measurement economics.* Having previously stipulated the existence of market equilibrium *and market-values* [in the form of exchange ratios] between pairs of commodities, Walras identifies an additional condition required for existence of equilibrium and market-value in the "general" sense.

> Under the conditions described above, there would indeed be a certain equilibrium in the market so far as the prices of commodities taken two at a time were concerned: but that equilibrium would be an imperfect equilibrium. *We do not have perfect or general market equilibrium unless the price of one of any two commodities in terms of the other is equal to the ratio of the prices of these two commodities in terms of any third commodity* [Walras, 1954, p. 157].

The condition which Walras states in italics is merely transitivity for the set of exchange ratios. It follows that Walras' "theorem of general equilibrium" is also a *theorem of market-value as a measurement order.* Lesson 11, in other words, is a story, true or false, not only about the duck, but about the rabbit as well.

b. The metrical structure problem

From Walras' time until ours, economics proceeded unquestioningly under the belief that, for an economy in general equilibrium, market-value exists as a simple *linear order* representable on a ratio scale whose defining standard may be either money or any of the commodities exchanged. A unit of any commodity, so goes traditional wisdom, can be adopted as the standard, and then all the other market-values in the economy can be expressed in terms of the market-value of quantities of that commodity. Market-value was assumed to have measurement properties analogous to those of length and mass, in that it was possible *in principle* to take units of any commodity, like bushels of wheat [Pigou, 1917], and combine them without limit in a way that is *additive* with respect to their market-value. According to this belief, the value of the aggregate endowment could be expressed as equal to the value of x units of any commodity.

Like most things pertaining to economics' measurement side, this notion about the structure of market-value, which seems not even to have a name, has become so much a part of the analytical woodwork that it also is not even recognized as a *hypothesis*. Economics' refusal to see, firstly, that **a measurement order's structure is empirically contingent**, and, second, that there exists both empirically and mathematically a diversity of such structures, owes much to *the failure to apply the relevant mathematics*. This omission may be due to an historical accident. Surely Walras, given his strong intuitive feel for the matter, would have applied the appropriate formalisms to the measurement side of his analysis if they had been available to him. Alas, they were not. In their place, he and his successors increasingly focused on the equilibrium side of his analysis, for which *homomorphic mathematical structures* were immediately at hand. In consequence, subsequent generations completely lost sight of the rabbit. This has led to three unexpected and potentially unsettling events: the homogeneity problem; Gary S. Becker's finding [Becker, 1962] that the law of demand holds irrespective of consumer rationality; and the more recent discovery that a numeraire can represent only a part of the market-value of the aggregate endowment.

The *first* event came when, on the heels of Keynes, general equilibrium theorists attempted to integrate money into their model. This gave rise to the notorious *homogeneity problem*: demands in the goods markets were homogeneous of degree zero in money prices, and the demand for money was homogeneous of degree one in money prices and the quantity of money. There followed attempts, some ingenious and all glorified with the name "synthesis", to patch over this horrific contradiction. Dealing with the discrepancy itself was not an option so long as theorists failed to see that this was a measurement problem, not an equilibrium one.

Monetary theory was founded on a hypothesis regarding the structure and measurement properties of market-value that differed fundamentally from general equilibrium's implicit theory of the same. At its most profound level, the quantity theory of money, from Locke onwards, is a set of *falsifiable* hypothesises about the structure of market-value as a measurement order. Among other things, the theory asserts that the market-value of the replicated standards of market-value measurement, i.e., units of money, varies in inverse proportion to the number of times such standards are used in market-value measurement operations, i.e. market exchange of an aggregate endowment. This, even by the standards of physical science, is a very strong proposition, as it not only asserts a functional relation, but also specifies the function. Furthermore, that this proposition is *synthetic rather than analytic* becomes obvious as soon as one considers other orders of direct measurement. The mass of standard weights, for example, is not affected by, let alone an inverse function of, the number of such weights used in a set of weighing operations.

In stating that *ceteris paribus*, a rate of variation x in the quantity of money exchanged varies the market-value of a unit of money by 1/1+x, the quantity theory of money asserts a hypothesis about the algebraic structure of market-value in a monetary economy. True, the quantity theory has identified this mathematically determinant property only with respect to money and at the macro level. But it would be rather astonishing if this unnamed "force" were not at work in more subtle ways with the market-values of commodities at the micro level. In any case, the 1/1+x property of market-value is not derivable from the notion of relative market-value from which Walras so elegantly derived his market-value theory. The notorious homogeneity problem arose because, with the rabbit lost to view, **economics had long operated with two different and**

incompatible theories of market-value. The one theory was based on an analysis beginning at the micro level, the other at the macro.

A *second* and now long forgotten surprise arising from the disregard of economics' measurement side occurred with the 1962 publication of a paper by Gary S. Becker. [Becker, 1962] He demonstrated that rationality was not a *necessary* condition for demand curves to slope downward to the right. Instead, the finiteness of funds available for expenditure is a *sufficient* condition for the law of demand to hold ultimately for every good. Although Becker's reasoning was incontrovertible and unchallenged, his discovery did not prove popular, and, despite its momentousness, was soon forgotten. Cynicism, it could be argued, accounted for the fate of Becker's finding, as it seemed to render a key part of economics' bread-and-butter analysis irrelevant. But another, more generous, explanation is possible: if one fails to see the metaphorical rabbit, one also will fail to see the positive theoretical implications of Becker's discovery.

Viewed under the measurement gestalt, *the law of demand is a type of non-additivity law for market-value.* It says that as the number of units of a commodity combined under market exchange operations is increased, the market-value of each unit will decrease and by the same amount. This law is of the same mathematical form as the market-value law that was found to be implicit in the traditional quantity theory. It differs only in that the rate of change x in the size of the commodity exchange set and the rate of change y in the unit market-value are not necessarily equal. (The conditions $x=y$, $x<y$ and $x>y$ correspond to the conditions of unitary, inelastic and elastic demand respectively.) It seems intuitively probable that *these two market-value laws*, one at the micro level and the other at the macro, are functionally interconnected *in a mathematically determinant way*. Thus, whereas Becker's discovery leads to a theoretical cul-de-sac *when viewed under the equilibrium gestalt*, it points immediately to a far-reaching theoretical connection when viewed under the measurement gestalt. In effect, Becker's 1962 paper was a preliminary exploration of *the interface of equilibrium and measurement economics*. But without an analytic repertoire that extended to measurement economics, he and his readers were unable to understand the theoretical significance of his discovery.

A *third* challenge to economics' implicit beliefs about the algebraic structure of market-value came in a paper I published in 1992 and appears as Appendix 2 in this book [Fullbrook, 1992]. Applying simple measurement theory, it proved the impossibility of ever representing more than half the market-value of the aggregate endowment when using a numeraire or standard commodity, and that in most cases the representable portion is but a tiny fraction of the aggregate's market-value. The significance of this discovery was not so much that it invalidated value form expressions of Walras' Law for a real economy (in fact the paper offered a way around this problem), but rather that the measurement order of market-value had *metrical properties* not previously suspected. More to the point, the 1992 revelation showed that Walras' heroic attempt to define metrically the notion of market-value **relative** to commodities in general is defective in some fundamental way.

6. Today we have no such excuse

It is a commonplace that modern economic theory has tended to drift free of any empirical anchorage [Fullbrook, 1994(b)]. Whereas in experimental sciences the failure to define precise *correspondence rules* ultimately condemns even the most dazzling analytical edifice to the dustbin, no such discipline holds in economics. Furthermore, whereas empirical findings and theoretical invention go hand in hand in the natural sciences, in economics the internal logic (analytic truth) of previously adopted and largely *uninterpreted formalisms* predestines theory development. Under such a regime, *the analytical lens inevitably tends to be mistaken for the object of inquiry.* These facts make the legacy of nineteenth-century economists an invaluable one. This chapter has tried to show how, along with their shortcomings, Mill, Walras and their contemporaries brought to *economic* phenomena a dexterity of thought which in our own more technically proficient age has been absent.

Economics' rabbit, history shows, is fleet of foot and, when sighted, heads for cover. Walras and succeeding generations failed to keep the rabbit in their sights because they lacked the analytical tools to do so. Today we have no such excuse.

Chapter 3

The metrical structure of market-value: $e_1' + e_2' \ldots + e_n' = 1$

Caution

Because of the tradition of pseudoscience in economics, there is the danger that the underlying nature of what follows will be fundamentally misunderstood. This chapter is in no way an effort at either axiomatic deduction or model-building; instead it is *a purely empirical endeavour.* How is this possible with just pen-and-paper? It is so because all quantitative orders, of which market-value is obviously one, have a structure. By making simple observations of the market-value world we live in, we can use elementary abstract algebra to *describe* market-value's metrical structure and thereby identify the category to which it belongs. And, as you will see, it turns out that it is not the one that for centuries we economists have presumed it to be.

1. Introduction

The traditional or neoclassical theory of value holds that the *quantitative order* called "market-value", or "exchange-value" is analysable into *intra*subjective preferences and ratios of exchange between pairs of commodities, and that market-values can be combined in a manner analogous to combining masses. This chapter will demonstrate:

1. that this presumed reducibility is logically impredicative;
2. that market-value is conditional upon and describes a broad *inter*subjective space;
3. that the structure of market-value is a relative quantity rather than an absolute one like length and mass;
4. that its algebraic structure is Boolean (The operators and axioms of Boolean algebra are set out on page 29 below);
5. that this Boolean structure, rather than the maximizing behavior of individual agents, accounts in the main for downward slopping demand curves; and
6. that some paradoxes that appeared in twentieth-century economic theory were due to applying absolute value assumptions to Boolean reality.

2. The nature of the beast

Length, time, mass, angular distance, probability, temperature and other measurement orders are characterized by various properties which together constitute a *structure*. These properties are open to description by elementary abstract algebra. That the metrical properties of these measurement orders – for example, mass, temperature and probability – diverge widely stands as common knowledge. So too does the fact that the Einsteinian revolution centred upon a reassessment of the metrics of fundamental orders of physical quantities. Previously, all physicists had assumed that lengths and masses could, in principle, be combined indefinitely in a manner analogous to lengths in a Euclidean space and to arithmetical operations on the set of real numbers.

Economics' failure to explore empirically the structure of market-value, its disregard of the possibility that its most basic presuppositions might not correspond to reality, is part of a once venerable intellectual tradition. Its greatest champion was Kant. In *The Critique of Pure Reason* he argued that it is possible to know some of reality's basic structures *a priori*, and he used every-day Euclidean notions of space and time as his central example. History, however, is cruel to *apriorism*, and never more so than with Kant's celebrated pronouncements on space and time. But economics has not yet escaped from subjective idealism as a way of thinking. Economists, with exceptions, do not permit empiricism to come between them and their *basic* concepts.

Yet that is what I propose to do for both you and me with respect to market-value. The parallel between the distinction that the following passage from Bertrand Russell describes and the one that this chapter is going to pursue is fairly exact.

> "Geometry", as we now know, is a name covering two different studies. On the one hand, there is pure geometry, which deduces consequences from axioms, without inquiring whether the axioms are "true"; this contains nothing that does not follow from logic, and is not "synthetic"... On the other hand, there is geometry as a branch of physics, as it appears, for example, in the general theory of relativity; this is an empirical science, in which *the axioms are inferred from measurements*, and are found to differ from Euclid's [emphasis added] [Russell, 1937, p. 688].

Economists, like physicists of an earlier age, share the general human weakness of *presuming that the world's deep structures resemble surface appearances*. For economics this means believing that every-day, common-sense understanding suffices for comprehending market-value's structure. Leaving this most fundamental of questions in the realm of pre-science or common-sense also gives the presumed answer the epistemological certainty demanded by economics' theoretical heritage.

3. The structure and methodology of this chapter

The argument develops in three stages. The first entertains a few fundamental questions about the minimum requirements for the establishment of market-value as a quantitative order. Prior to Walras it was common to regard market-value, like probability, as a *relational* property – not one that holds for commodities individually as do mass and extension for physical objects. But then what exactly are the terms of the market-value relation? And how many are required for its existence? John Stuart Mill's assertion that market-value is reducible to a relation between market agents and two commodities will be tested for logical coherence. The second and main stage of the argument considers what various commonly observed market phenomena infer about the structure of market-value. The third stage considers the broad implications of the results of stages one and two, and shows that several major theoretical anomalies that surfaced in the twentieth century result from economics' misunderstandings of the structure of market-value.

Four aspects of this chapter's methodology need foregrounding.

First, and most important, the method is Newton's "experimental philosophy" or what Tony Lawson calls *retroduction* [Lawson, 1997]. Economists accustomed only to working with the deductive method – as described by Russell above – will be predisposed to read this chapter inside-out, making it appear that I have indulged in a bizarre selection of axioms to produce a whimsical Escher-like landscape. But such an error is easily avoided by grasping one crucial point. *This chapter's logical inferences proceed from the level of observable phenomena back to the level of underlying structures or "axioms" in Russell's second sense of the word.* The goal is to discover, not the properties of an axiom system, but rather those of *a particular real-life system of relations*, the market price system. In lieu of economics' traditional axioms, the argument begins on the basis of a presumption of possibility, namely, that, just as the objective character of lightning is not exhausted by its visual appearance, so it is unlikely that the structure of market-value reveals itself fully in the situation of everyday market exchange. Given the long hegemony of *apriorism* in this field, little, in fact, is known about the metrical structure of market-value. This chapter will show that its structure is more highly defined than previously thought.

Second, the *structure*'s explanatory significance must be clarified. As noted above, structure plays a foundational role in Equilibrium Economics, (EE) explanation. But because EE's assumption regarding the structure of market-value performs its function unnoticed, it has been possible to foster the myth that EE conclusions have been reached solely on the basis of axiomatic generalizations about individual behaviour. If inquiry reveals that the metric of market-value is not the metric assumed, then the theorizing of market-value must begin afresh.

Third, beliefs regarding the structure of market-value as a quantitative order tend to be folkloric. This book aims to break with that tradition and bring the question of market-value's structure into the realm of science. This means looking for and at **empirical** evidence as to market-value's structure. How is this possible? It is possible because all real-world measurement orders – e.g. mass, length, velocity, angle and temperature – have metrical structures (metrics) **whose existence is completely independent of axioms and other speculations.**[1] Like all empirical phenomena, these structures are potentially open to *description*. Description consists of language, one category of which is mathematics and whose abstract algebra is especially suitable for ***describing*** the metrical structures of measurement orders. Because as economists we have become so accustomed to beginning our theorizing with assumptions rather than descriptions, I will first *describe* the metric of mass. I will then use identical procedures to *describe* the metric of market-value. These descriptions entail only elementary abstract algebra, whose use will be kept to a minimum and paralleled with verbal descriptions. Ultimately we are looking for a homomorphism between an *empirical* relational system and a numerical relational system. If my audience consisted of natural scientists, my next sentence would be unneeded. This homomorphism if found, will be so by finding a numerical relational system that fits the observed empirical one, rather than by making

[1] It is these measurement orders with their *empirically* identified metrics that constitute the primary foundation upon which theoretical physics has been built.

"assumptions" about the empirical system so that it fits a numerical one.

Fourth, this chapter's analysis proceeds on the assumption that there are only income exchangeables, and thus the term "aggregate endowment" does not include asset exchangeables. But in Chapter 4 the analysis will be expanded to include asset exchangeables.

4. The empirical observations

So, what are the promised empirical observations on the basis of which this chapter will proceed? There are five of them, and none are contentious.[2]

1. (E3) Exchangeables have downward sloping demand curves.
2. (E4, E5, E6) The demand for some exchangeables is inelastic.
3. (E7) The market-value of an exchangeable refers to how much of something else it exchanges for in a market.
4. (E8) Increasing (decreasing) the quantity of money exchanged for the aggregate endowment decreases (increases) the market-value of the money unit.
5. (E9, E10) Increasing (decreasing) the quantity of money exchanged for the aggregate endowment does *not* change the aggregate endowment's market-value.

---

[2] The numbered Es in parenthesis refer to the algebraic expressed propositions (stated below in sections 8, 9, 10 and 12) which the observation entails.

We are going to translate these five empirical observations into the language of abstract algebra. These translations will then reveal a metrical structure. And although it turns out to be a well-known metric, it is not the one upon which Equilibrium Economics has been constructed.

5. Testing the notion of market-value as a relation between two exchangeables for logical coherence

Can market-value be identified as originating with or shown to be reducible to a set of relations between pairs of objects? The following passage from Alfred Marshall identifies market or exchange value as based on a relative concept, one holding between pairs of commodities.

> The value, that is the exchange value, of one thing in terms of another at any place and time, is the amount of that second thing which can be got there and then in exchange for the first. Thus, the term value is relative, and *expresses the relation between two things* at a particular place and time [emphasis added] [Marshall, 1920, p. 61].

To give it every possible chance, I want to formulate this notion of relative market-value more precisely before seeing if it holds up to logical analysis. Thus:

> For pairs of commodities, there is the exchange-value of each commodity *relative to the other*, in the sense that quantities of the two commodities are said to be equal in value if they exchange for each other and to change in value

> if there is a change in the pair's market-clearing exchange ratio [*ibid*].

This reformulation, as well as Marshall's sentence, appears coherent. But the twentieth century discovered that the logical relations of statements are not always what they appear to be. So I am going to test the stated notion of relative market-value against the general principle that, *between any two magnitudes of the same empirical order, an equality relation either holds or does not.* Consider two commodities *X* and *Y*, and whose units are *x* and *y*. Let *a*, *b*, and *σ* be rational positive numbers.

Assume that the initial market-clearing ratio of *ax:by* changes to *ax:σby*. Then, according to Marshall's concept of relative market-value, the market-values of quantities of *X* relative to *Y* have changed. Any two quantities of the same order are either equal or not equal. Therefore, the market-value *of σby relative to X* at the new exchange ratio is either equal or not equal to the exchange value *of by* at the old exchange ratio.

First assume that the market-values of *σby* and *by* are equal. Then, because at the old ratio the market-values of *ax* and *by* were equal and at the new ratio the market-values of *ax* and *σby* are equal, it follows that the market-value of *ax* is unchanged. This contradicts the assumption that the market-values of quantities of *X* relative to *Y* have changed, and so one must conclude that this case cannot obtain.

Assume the other possibility: the market-value of *σby* at the new exchange ratio is not equal to the market-value of *by* at the old exchange ratio. If, relative to *X*, *by* and *σby* are not equal in market-value, then by Marshall's concept of relative market-value they do not exchange for the same number of units of *X*. However, by assumption they do exchange for the same number of units of *X*. Therefore, this case also cannot obtain. And this exhausts the logical possibilities.

Marshall's concept of relative market-value generates paradoxes because it is circular. It defines a commodity's market-value in terms of the market-value of a second commodity whose market-value is defined in terms of the market-value of the first. In technical terms, this constitutes "vicious circularity" which renders the definition impredicative.

This simple but unexpected outcome of the test for logical coherence shows that, as a quantitative order, market-value has unexpected properties. Whereas the traditional but impredicative notion of market-value reduced to the field of two atomistic agents – two independent subjectivities – making an exchange, we now know that the minimal field for existence of market-value must be larger. It is premature to ponder what this might mean. Doing so now would risk perplexity. First, we must pursue other possibilities for analysis and hope that with further results all will become clear.

6. False resemblances

Confusions, like the one unearthed in the previous section, come easily when thinking about market-value because in two respects it bears a false similarity to familiar physical magnitudes.

First, the notion of market-value as a relation between two

commodities exhibits a superficial resemblance to the comparing two masses or two lengths to each other. These physical concepts, however, are not predicated as relations between individual masses and lengths. *It is only their measurement numbers that are conceived in this way.* Instead, Newtonian physics predicates mass and extension as properties possessed by bodies independently of their relations to other bodies. This independence saves the quantitative concepts of length and mass from impredicativeness [Carnap, 1966, pp. 51-61].

Second, and related to the first, although market-value numbers are expressed on a ratio scale like mass and length numbers, they are generated in a profoundly different manner. Physical measurement numbers refer to physical phenomena, called concrete quantities, which have been found to have a structure homomorphic to the system of units and numbers (abstract quantities) by which they are represented. A cardinal point is that these concrete physical quantities do not come into being as the result of humankind's invention of processes of numerically representing them. If a means of numerically representing the weight of your body had never been invented, you would experience its weight all the same. The existence of the properties of extension and mass are independent of the processes by which they are measured or compared. In contrast, *the quantitative order of market-value does not exist independently of the process which assigns market-value numbers.* Without market exchange there is no exchange or market value. Market exchange, in other words, is the process by which the market-value order, not just the numbers which describe it, comes into being.

The fact that the process that determines concrete market-values also assigns numbers to represent them invites conflation of *concrete market-values* and *market-value numbers*. The latter, stripped of their units, belong to *R*, the set of positive reals which defines a Euclidean space. Thus, *the conflation of concrete and abstract market-values* leads smoothly to the unsupported conclusion that a "price space" is a Euclidean space [Debreu, 1986, p. 1261].

It is on the basis of this presumed "fit of the mathematical form to the economic content" [Debreu, 1986, p. 1259] that the whole EE edifice, not just general equilibrium theory, has been constructed. At every point it presumes – through the convenience of its conflation – that a system of exchange or market values has the same structural properties, i.e., Euclidean, as do the numbers that represent them. But this subconscious presumption, *the most fundamental hypothesis of Equilibrium Economics* , is easily tested when the conflation between concrete and abstract quantities is avoided.

Traditionally in economics when the words "structure" and "market" appear close together, one is referring to market structures in the sense of perfect competition, imperfect competition, oligopoly, and monopoly. This is not the case in what follows. Instead, when the term "structure" is used it refers to *metrical orders*, usually market-value.

7. Test procedure

"How many snowballs would be required to heat an oven?" [Duhem, 1905, p. 112]. This joke, credited to Diderot, illustrates three verities of quantitative science: profound structural differences exist between various quantitative orders; their structures may diverge radically from that of ordinary arithmetic; and, most importantly, the structures of empirical quantitative orders are autonomous *vis-à-vis* human will and imagination.

In a more positive vein, but to a similar purpose, Bertrand Russell identified the principle by which science applies mathematics to empirical phenomena.

> "Whenever two sets of terms have mutual relations of the same type, the same form of deduction will apply to both" [Russell, 1937, p. 7].

Application of arithmetical addition to mass, length and time are familiar examples. Yet, in such cases, where one set of terms is logical or mathematical and the other set is not, the existence of a homomorphism between the two sets is, as Diderot's jest illustrates,

> *a purely empirical matter.* It presumes the discovery of a set of *extra-mathematical relations* which repeated testing, *not* a set of axioms, shows to be structurally analogous to the set of mathematical relations.

Monetarized markets assign to each set of commodities exchanged a denominate number describing a property – the "market-value" or "exchange-value" – of that set. It is, therefore, although unorthodox, eminently sensible, and as explained in Chapter 2, *to examine those exchanges as measurement operations.* But the rarity of this approach and its false resemblance to demand theory's axiomatic method, makes it wise to begin by outlining and illustrating, even at the risk of labouring the obvious, *the general empirical principles* involved. For this purpose I will consider in some detail the procedures, and the logic behind them, for measurement of mass.

A loaded scale in level balance defines operationally a symmetrical, transitive and reflexive relation $=_m$ between a pair of masses. This physical relation, $=_m$, is an archetypal empirical equivalence relation. Similarly, a scales out of level balance defines the asymmetrical, transitive, and irreflexive precedence relations lighter than $<_m$ and heavier than $>_m$. I am particularly concerned with the property, or absence of, additivity, and with the fact that physics attributes this property to mass, not on the basis of any axiom or axiom set, but rather on the basis of the results of empirical operations. It is only after equivalence and precedence relations and a numerical scale have been developed and tested for a domain of objects that it becomes possible to *test* for additivity. This property, it must be emphasized, never holds absolutely for elements of a measurement order. Instead, additivity holds only relative to *some particular mode of combination*. Lengths, for example, are additive only when combined end-to-end in a straight line perpendicular to the axis of gravity. With the measurement of mass, the combining operation is merely the joint positioning of two objects in a pan of a scales and weighing them as a single object. In general, where $\bigcirc$ denotes an empirical combining operation and *p* the measurement number assigned to the object in the parenthesis, the additivity condition may be stated:

$$p(a \bigcirc b) = p(a) + p(b).$$

For mass, this condition is interpreted as follows. One puts object *a* on one of the pans of a scales which then is brought into balance with standard weights whose mass number m is observed. Object *a* is then replaced with object *b* and its mass is noted. Then the two objects are placed together on the scale, this being the combining operation for mass $\oplus$, and the measurement number of the combined mass is determined. From experience, one predicts that the mass number of *a* and *b* combined will be the arithmetical sum of the mass numbers of *a* and *b* weighed separately, i.e.,

$$m(a \oplus b) = m(a) + m(b).$$

With respect to the equivalence and precedence relations $=_m$, $<_m$ and $>_m$, and the operation of combining masses in the pans of a scales, the physical order of mass satisfies not only the additivity condition, but also a set of conditions structurally analogous to those satisfied by arithmetical addition in the set of positive real numbers $\underline{R}^+$. *Arithmetical addition* + together with the arithmetical relations =, < and > satisfy the following conditions for any elements x, y, z of $\underline{R}^+$.

A1. $x + (y + z) = (x + y) + z$ (associativity).

A2. $x + y = y + x$ (commutativity).

A3. $z + x = z + y$ implies $x = y$ (cancellation property of + with respect to =).

A4. $(z + x) < (z + y)$ implies $x < y$ (cancellation property of + with respect to <).

A5. $(x + y) > x$ (monoticity).

A6. For any x and y there exists an integer n such that $nx > y$ (Archimedean property).

Where $=_p$, $<_p$ and $>_p$ denote unspecified empirical equivalence and precedence relations for a property P, $\bigcirc$ an unspecified empirical combining operation, and a,b,c are elements of the set S of all objects possessed of the property P, then the empirical conditions corresponding to A1–A6 are as follows.

P1. $a \bigcirc (b \bigcirc c) =_p (a \bigcirc b) \bigcirc c$
P2. $a \bigcirc b =_p b \bigcirc a$.
P3. $c \bigcirc a =_p c \bigcirc b$ implies $a =_p b$
P4. $c \bigcirc a <_p c \bigcirc b$ implies $a <_p b$
P5. $a \bigcirc b >_p a$.
P6. For any a such that $a =_p a_1 =_p a_2 =_p \ldots =_p a_n$ and any b there is an nth power $a \bigcirc a \bigcirc \ldots \bigcirc a$ of a, written na, such that $na >_p b$.

It is important to note that the conditions P1–P6 refer to relations holding between *empirical objects*, not between measurement numbers describing those objects. But where an empirical order such as mass has been metricated – that is, where an easily reproducible object or process possessing the property has been chosen as a standard for defining a unit of that property – conditions corresponding to P1–P6 can be expressed in terms of measurement numbers and *arithmetical*, rather than empirical, relations. The P' list that follows includes as *P'3* the basic *additivity condition* noted above. Thus, where **p** denotes the measurement number assigned to the object in the parenthesis, we have:

P'1. $p(a \bigcirc (b \bigcirc c) = p(a \bigcirc b) \bigcirc c$
P'2. $p(a \bigcirc b) = p(b \bigcirc a)$
P'3. $p(a \bigcirc b) = p(a) + p(b)$
P'4. $p(c \bigcirc a) = p(c \bigcirc b)$ implies $p(a) = p(b)$
P'5. $p(c \bigcirc a) < p(c \bigcirc b)$ implies $p(a) < p(b)$
P'6. $p(a \bigcirc b) > p(a)$

P'7. For any a such that $p(a) = p(a_1) = p(a_2) = \ldots = p(a_n)$ and any b there is a nth power $a \bigcirc a \bigcirc \ldots \bigcirc a$ of a, written na, such that $p(na) > p(b)$.

We will use these P' conditions to guide the inquiry into the structural characteristics of market-value. Each P' condition generates a question to ask about market-value: Does market-value satisfy condition P'x, and if not, what corresponding condition does it satisfy? To answer these questions requires that various aspects of market-value are examined from the structural point of view. These include

- market exchange as a measurement operation,
- downward sloping demand curves,
- inelastic demand,
- market-value units and, eventually,
- monetary inflation.

In this way the investigation reveals a set of structural properties of market-value paralleling the P' conditions. This method of proceeding also has the advantage of placing the concrete structural properties of market-value in direct comparison to a structure, P'1-P'7, made commonplace through length and mass measurement. First the operational basis of market-value measurement must be explained.

8. Market-value as a measurement phenomenon

This chapter draws heavily on measurement theory, especially Campbell 1928, Ellis 1966, Feather 1959, Hempel 1952, Krantz et al. 1971 and Menger 1959. Familiarity with measurement theory is uncommon amongst economists, a lack that has enabled the publication of a few economics papers purporting to be on this subject and which are shockingly philistine.

When considering a homomorphism between a set of logical or mathematical relations and a set of empirical relations, it is important not to conflate the two realms. The measurement numbers that describe a set of empirical relations are accurate only up to some degree, or, in other words, all are inaccurate to some degree. Furthermore, the degree of inaccuracy varies enormously between different orders and within the same order between different centuries and different measuring conditions. Market-value is no exception. Measurement inaccuracies mean that the measurement numbers, for example length numbers, will not *perfectly* satisfy the set of mathematical relations, for examples P1 . . . P6 as above and E1 . . . E10 as below, to which the empirical order is homomorphic. Although this discrepancy between description of abstract phenomena and description of real-world phenomena is part of the eternal nature of advanced empirical science, it is easily misinterpreted as faulty reasoning by someone whose thinking has for decades been conditioned by *a priori* theorising.

Homomorphic thinking can be especially precarious when considering market-value because, as explained in Chapter 2, market-value differs from other quantitative orders in that it comes into existence only through its measurement process. Therefore, measurement irregularities affect concrete instances of the empirical order itself and, as will be exampled in Chapter 5, motivate their occurrence. But just as interferences with rolls of the dice do not change the metrical structure of probability, so also market manipulations and other historical irregularities do not change the metrical structure of market-value.

Everyday usage, and that of many economists, fails to differentiate between quantities of *things* and quantities of *measurement*. But in science, as noted in the previous chapter, the distinction between these two kinds of denominate numbers is fundamental. By definition, numbers of count have reference only to particular classes of objects. This property severely limits the scientific significance of count numbers, even when their units are based on measurable properties, for example, a pound of butter. Instead, it is the quantification of *properties* common to many classes of objects (for example, mass, length, time and market-value) which enables the generation of quantitative laws and of theoretical structures which transcend Aristotelian categories.

Just as mass and extension are properties common to all physical objects, so market-value is a property of all economic objects. It is on this basis that market-value must be judged a measurement order. But it is an extremely curious one, because, as noted in Chapter 2, the process of market-value measurement, that is, market exchange, is an integral and central part of economics' object of inquiry. Nevertheless, market-value, like the fundamental measurement orders of classical physics, is operationally defined in terms of a combining operation, a measurement object, an equivalence relation and a pair of precedence relations. Each of these elements of market-value measurement needs examination.

a. The combining operation

In a time period T, various categories of goods are exchanged for money in markets. In each of these markets, the placement in period T of multiple units of a good for exchange constitutes the *empirical combining operation* $\odot$ for the measurement of market-value, just as the simultaneous placement of multiple objects on a scales for weighing defines the combining operation $\oplus$ for the measurement of mass.

b. The measurement object

Physical objects combined under $\oplus$ for weighing constitute the "object mass"; similarly, the units of a commodity X combined under $\odot$ constitute X's *market exchange or measurement set* for period T.

c. The equivalence and precedence relations

The market conditions of equilibrium and disequilibrium serve as equivalence and precedence relations for the measurement of market-value. A market which clears and is in equilibrium defines a *market-value equivalence relation* $=_e$ such that the market-value of the quantity of a good exchanged equals the market-value of the quantity of money exchanged for it. This relation parallels the equivalence relation used in weighing. When a loading of a scales results in a level equilibrium, the object mass is said to be equal to the combined mass of the mass standards ("weights") placed in the opposite pan.

Still another parallel exists between mass and market-value measurement. In market trading, as in weighing, equilibrium is reached through trial and error. The initial price set for a commodity may or may not result in a market equilibrium, just as the initial number of units of standard mass placed in one pan may or may not result in an equilibrium of the scales.

As with the measurement of mass, the conditions of associativity and commutativity appear to hold for market-value by definition. Thus, where *e* denotes the market-value **number** assigned to the homogeneous commodity set in parentheses:

E1. e(a ⊙ (b ⊙ c)) = e((a ⊙ b) ⊙ c).
E2. e(a ⊙ b) = e(b ⊙ a).

9. The law of demand as a law of negative non-additivity

Despite the structural similarities between the measuring of mass and the measuring of market-value, the *numerical results* of the two sets of operations are structurally dissimilar. This disparity becomes obvious once the negative slope of commodity demand curves is interpreted in terms of the additivity condition. *If market-values were additive relative to their measurement combining operation, then all demand curves would be horizontal.* A demand curve's slope means that as additional units of the commodity are placed on the market for exchange, ⊙, their market-value is not additive. Moreover, the fact that a demand curve slopes downward means that market-value is negatively non-additive in the following sense. On the basis of experiential knowledge of market exchange, one can predict: for a given demand, that the market-value of homogeneous commodity sets ***a*** and ***b*** combined into one market exchange set will be less than the arithmetical sum of the market-values of ***a*** and ***b*** if they are exchanged separately in different periods. Thus, where $\underline{e}$ denotes the market-value number assigned to the market exchange set of commodity X in the parenthesis:

E3. $e(a \odot b) < e(a) + e(b)$.

10. Inelastic demand

This section continues with the deployment of the properties P'1-P'7, which describe the structure of metricated empirical orders analogous to arithmetical addition in $\underline{R}^+$, as heuristic devices for identifying the structural properties of market-value. I wish to discover how the phenomenon of *inelastic demand* relates to the properties

P'4. $p(c \bigcirc a) = p(c \bigcirc b)$ implies $p(a) = p(b)$
P'5. $p(c \bigcirc a) < p(c \bigcirc b)$ implies $p(a) < p(b)$
P'6. $p(a \bigcirc b) > p(a)$.

The previous section showed how the inverse relation between price and quantity demanded means that, *over the operation of market exchange, market-value is non-additive.* Inelastic demand identifies a situation in which market-value is not only non-additive, but "negatively" so, in the sense that increasing the size of the market exchange set *decreases* its market-value. This condition generates relations which violate conditions P'4, P'5 and P'6.

I begin by considering P'6, because the inconsistency of inelastic demand with this property is self-evident. Interpreted in terms of market-value, inelasticity of demand means that beyond a certain size, the larger a commodity's market exchange set, the less its market-value. Formally, when the demand for a commodity is inelastic or unitary and the sets in parenthesis are market exchange sets of the commodity, we have:

$$e(a \odot b) \leq e(a),$$

which is contrary to P'6. On the other hand, when the demand for the commodity is elastic:

$$e(a \odot b) > e(a).$$

Therefore the following relation characterizes market-value:

E6. $e(a \odot b) >, = \text{ or } < e(a)$.

Inelastic demand's inconsistency with conditions P'4 and P'5 *vis-à-vis* market-value and the operation of market exchange is only slightly less obvious. It is illustrated, in Figures 1 and 2 on the following page, by a curve which I will call a "total market-value curve". It plots changes in a commodity's market exchange set's size to changes in that set's market-value. In other words, the total market-value curve shows how, as the number of units of a commodity traded in a period of time changes, the market value of that total changes.

In Figures 1 and 2, a, b, and c stand for quantities (or sets) of the market's commodity, whereas the quantities in parentheses stand for *market exchange sets*, that is the total quantity of the commodity exchanged in period T. Figure 1 shows that the market exchange sets of $(c \odot a)$ and $(c \odot b)$ have the same market-value, but that the market-value of the market exchange set (a) is less than the market-value of that of (b). This violates condition P'4. Instead of P'4, the following relation characterizes, market-value:

E4. $e(c \odot a) = e(c \odot b)$ does not imply $e(a) = e(b)$.

Figure 1 Total market-value curve for commodity X
e(c ⊙ a) = e(c ⊙ b), but e(b) < e(a), where a = 20 units, b = 80 units and c = 15 units

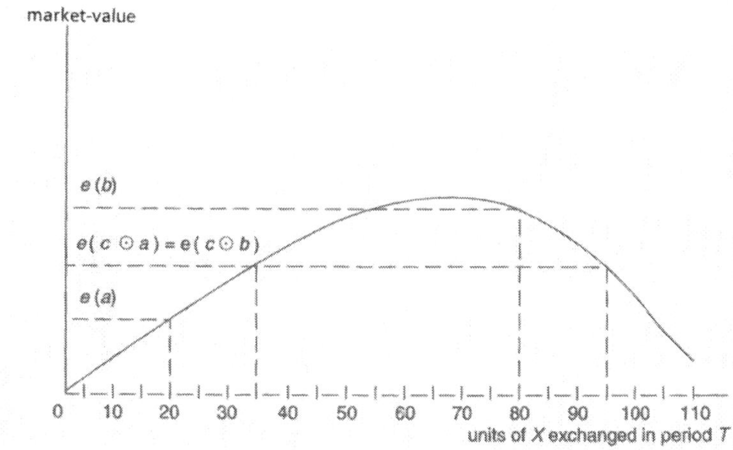

Figure 2 Total market-value curve for commodity Y
e(c ⊙ a) < e(c ⊙ b), but e(a) > (e(b), where a = 80 units, b = 30 units and c = 30 units

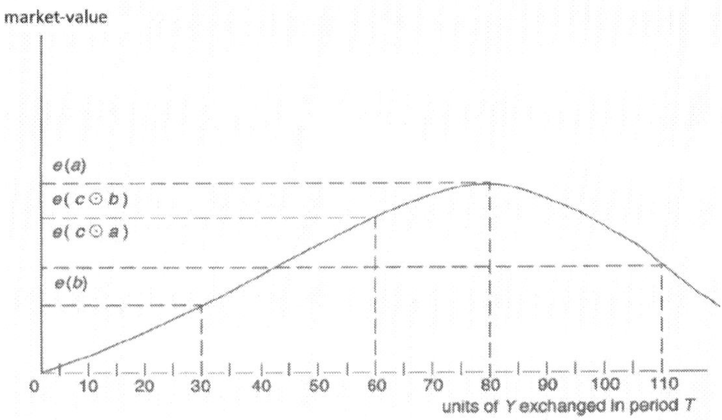

Figure 2 shows that the market-value of the market exchange set of (c ⊙ a) is less than that of (c ⊙ b), despite the fact that the market-value of (a) is greater than that of (b). This violates condition P'5. Instead of P'5, the following relation characterizes market-value:

E5. $e(c \odot a) < e(c \odot b)$ does not imply $e(a) < e(b)$.

Thus, the existence of inelastic demand means that the conditions P'4, P'5 and P'6 do not hold for market-value.

11. The commensurability problem with units of account

A unit ratio scale[3] representation of a quantitatively structured *property P*, such as mass or market-value, is constructed with a unit of the property defined on the basis of some object or process characterized by P and called the standard [Campbell, 1928; Hempel, 1952; Feather, 1959; Carnap, 1966; Ellis, 1966; Krantz, 1971]. But given the creation of such a scale, there still remains the empirical question of that scale's range of magnitude relative to that of the property to whose measurement it is applied. Existence of a unit ratio scale representation system across a property's full range of magnitudes, a "complete" as opposed to only a "partial" scale, means it is possible in principle to *combine* enough copies of the standard to make it P-commensurable, $=_p$, with every object in the domain [Hempel, pp. 62-8]. This corresponds to a weak version of the Archimedean conditions A6 and P6 and P'7 of Section 6.

[3] Although unconventional, in this context to avoid possible confusion I will use the term "unit ratio scale" rather than "ratio scale", given that when a quantitative order possesses two fixed points, for example probability, there may be unit-less scales that are technically ratio scales.

When working with "real" models, economics concerns itself tangentially with the process of constructing a system of representation, including a scale, for market-value. Without money, it is necessary to adopt a commodity as a numeraire; and, regarding such designations, Pigou [1917] summed up what has remained the traditional wisdom regarding money-value's satisfaction of an Archimedean condition. In "The Value of Money" Pigou declared, "the value of any combination of commodities in general can be cited in terms of any single commodity". This "Pigou Hypothesis" may be stated formally for the aggregate endowment Γ as follows, where "a" is the standard unit of a commodity *A* and $\geq_e$ means equal or greater than in market-value.

For any *A* and any Γ there is potentially a nth power of a ⊙ a ⊙ ... ⊙ a of a, written

na, such that na $\geq_e$ Γ.

Further thought, however, shows that not only is Pigou's hypothesis false, but also that there is no single commodity and only one combination of commodities in terms of which the value of the aggregate endowment can be cited. The argument by which this result is reached is disconcertingly simple. Just as a physical object only has weight in a gravitational field, so too a good only has market-value in the context of a system of markets, with its "forces" of supply and demand. If a good's market-value were equal to the market-value of the aggregate endowment, then it would be the only good in the endowment, in which case there would be no demand, no exchanges, no market and no market-value. A similar contradiction arises when it is assumed that the equilibrium market-value of a quantity of a good is more than half the value of the aggregate endowment. This structural attribute of market-value may be expressed formally as follows, where, as above, Γ indicates the aggregate endowment, "a" the standard unit of a commodity *A*, and $\geq_e$ means equal or greater than in market-value:

> E7. For any Γ there is no *A* such that there is a nth power of a ⊙ a ⊙ ... ⊙ a of a, written na, such that the market-value of na is more than half the market-value of Γ.

A corollary of E7 is that for any commodity there must be a quantity beyond which its demand ceases to be elastic, or, from this book's point of view, beyond which the market-value of the commodity's market exchange set does not increase.

This obstacle to a full representation of market-value in a real economy can be overcome if and only if the aggregate endowment Γ is adopted as the standard of market-value. Under such a system, market-values would be represented as proportionate *parts of the whole market-value*, in the same way that probabilities are conceived and expressed as fractional parts of a certainty or of the universal event. These peculiarities of representing market-value in a real economy are further indications of market-value's idiosyncratic structure.

12. Monetary inflation

In all that follows:

- "money" includes money *in all its contemporary forms*, and
- M = the quantity of money *exchanged* in period t.

Monetary inflation may be commonplace, but as a measurement phenomenon it is eccentric. Consider mass. Increasing the number of standard weights used in weighing operations does not decrease the mass of those weights. Likewise, increasing the number of standard rods used in measuring length does not change the length of any of those rods. But increasing the quantity of money exchanged, that is, the number of standards of market-value used in measuring the market-value of the component sets of the aggregate endowment – not only decreases the market-value of existing money, it also decreases each unit's value by the same proportion. This shows that, in still another way, market-value has a metrical structure radically different from mass, length and arithmetical addition.

Consider further the case of mass. The property of mass is understood as a function of micromasses, whose existences are independent of the larger mass with which they are grouped. A body's mass is the totality of the masses of that body's parts, and its mass will increase if more parts are added to it. With quantitative properties of this type, each magnitude is *the aggregate of its parts, the direction of determination running from the micro to the macro level.*

But quantitative properties are not always of this type. Probability provides a relevant example. Certainty not only defines an upper bound for magnitudes of probability, but also serves as a whole in relation to which the probabilities of events in the probability space are conceived as parts. In other words, certainty, or the certain event, provides a *unique* standard of measurement for probability, with all other probabilities in the space existing only as parts of that "whole" probability. In this sense, just as the existence of a mass is based on *a sum of its parts relation*, an event's probability is based on *a part of a whole relation.*

As a means of gaining insight into the structure of market-value and its relation to money, consider the case of an uniform probability space, such as drawing from a deck of cards. Under the concept of probability, each card in the deck shares equally in *the "whole" probability*, that is, the certainty that when a card from a deck is drawn one of the *n* cards in the deck will be drawn. Changing the number of cards in the deck changes each card's probability of being drawn, but does not change the probability of the certain event. Furthermore, despite the change in the number of elementary events, and the change in every card's probability of being drawn, the sum of their probabilities remains equal to the probability of the certain event, and each card's probability remains equal to every other card's probability. *A formally identical set of relations holds for the market-value of money.* It is generally agreed that an increase or decrease in the number of units of money exchanged for the aggregate endowment Γ, although altering the market-value of every unit of money, and thereby *changing the scale on which market-values are represented*, does not change the market-value of Γ, nor disturb the equality between the market-value of M and the market-value of Γ, nor eliminate the market-value equivalency between all the individual money units. These relations are loaded with structural significance, and so need to be added to the list of market-value's metrical properties. Where *m* is a unit of money, *n* is the numeric of M (i.e., nm = M), Γ is the aggregate endowment, each of whose elements is exchanged only once, and all markets clear, the following relations describe operational aspects of market-value measurement.

E8. The market-value of Γ is constant for all magnitudes of M.
E9. For any (numerical) value of M, $M =_e \Gamma$.
E10. Where nm = M, for any value of n, $m =_e M/n$.

We need to consider further these relations.

Money affords a unique analytical opportunity, because with it the usual order of dependency between use-value and market-value is reversed. Money has use-value only *because it has market-value.*[4] This reversal provides a case where the market-values of a homogenous set of objects are determined independently of multifarious use-value considerations. For this reason, money offers a much clearer view of the structure of market-value than the one had from looking at the market-value of commodities.

Of special interest are the properties of the relations by which the market system causes definite magnitudes of market-value to become associated with (i.e., become a property of) the money units. Most of all, it is important to note *the direction of determination.* Is the market-value of M determined by the number and the market-value of the money units composing M, that is, a ***micro→macro explanation***, or is the market-value of the individual units of

[4] The demand for money is a pure case of the type of market situation analysed by the French Intersubjectivists. See Dupuy, 1989; Levy, 1991, 1994; Orléan, 1990, 1992; and most especially 1998. See also Fullbrook, 1994b, 1996b.

money determined by the number of parts into which the market-value of M is divided, that is, a ***macro→micro explanation***? If the market exchange process assigns a market-value directly to the standard money unit, then the market-value of M would be *directly* proportional to M. But if the primary assignment of market-value is to the total quantity of money exchanged, whatever its magnitude, then the market-value of the money unit would be *inversely* proportional to M. The existence of *inflation*, as described above, shows that it is the latter process which characterizes market-value and money. The market-value of the total quantity of money exchanged equals that of the goods for which it exchanges, or, in an economy where all markets clear, the market-value of the aggregate endowment of goods (E9). This means that it is the aggregate endowment that is , like certainty is for probability, the primary reference point for the quantitative order we call market-value (E8), with the market-value of the money units being determined as *equal parts* of the aggregate endowment's market-value (E10).

This inverse relation between the quantity of money and the market-value of its units corresponds to the negative non-additive law derived earlier with respect to the market-value of commodities (E3). But here, with the market-value of money, is a very special or pure case of this law, pure in the sense that it is characterized by a fully specified and invariant function – the rarest of all phenomena in the social sciences. Other things remaining unchanged, a percentage change x in the quantity of money exchanged decreases the market-value of a unit of money by 1/1+x. In other words, for a given Γ, a money unit's elasticity of market-value with respect to quantity of money exchanged is unitary, that is, a constant.

This section has used the empirical phenomenon of inflation to reveal the structure of the economic process by which money comes to have the property of market-value. If, as with most quantitative orders, the determination of magnitude proceeded from the part to the whole, then an increase in the quantity of money exchanged would not only increase the market-value of M, but would also leave the market-value of the monetary units unchanged. In such a world, monetary inflation would be impossible. Instead, other things being equal, increasing M affects the market-value of individual money units in the same way as increasing the number of elementary events in an equiprobable probability space affects each of those events' probability.

13. Summary of the metrical properties of market-value discovered

This chapter's results thus far spring from two simple but novel analytical manoeuvres: raising the question "What is the metric of market-value?" and undertaking an analysis of the market system as a measurement system. This dual strategy affords a fresh analytical point of view on a much observed and often analysed set of phenomena. Old verities and celebrated results may be scrutinized and further examined within the context of this new but complementary **analytical framework**. Thus, *the law of demand (in the empirical sense of an observed regularity), is now interpreted as a law of negative non-additivity of market-value.* Likewise, from relations expressed in the equation of exchange, a fully specified law of negative non-additivity of market-value has been derived for money. Because of the failure to look at price and quantity phenomena from the measurement and

structural angles, *these non-additivity laws, despite their simplicity, have not previously entered economic thought.*
The *metric and measurement approach* also raised questions about the representation of market-value, questions whose answers have not been backed previously by analysis. In considering this set of questions, it has been found that the commensurability condition in a real economy is satisfiable only if market-values are represented as fractional parts of the whole market-value, that is, the market-value of the aggregate endowment. Furthermore, it also is the aggregate endowment's market-value which serves as the primary standard of market-value in a monetary economy, with the market-value of the individual money units depending on *the number of parts into which the whole market-value is divided.*

There follows a list of the structural properties of market-value as a measurement order discovered thus far.

E1. $e(a \odot (b \odot c)) = e((a \odot b) \odot c)$.

E2. $e(a \odot b) = e(b \odot a)$.

E3. $e(a \odot b) < e(a) + e(b)$.

E4. $e(c \odot a) = e(c \odot b)$ does not imply $e(a) = e(b)$.

E5. $e(c \odot a) < e(c \odot b)$ does not imply $e(a) < e(b)$.

E6. $e(a \odot b)$ >, = or < $e(a)$.

E7. For any Γ there is no A such that there is a nth power of $a \odot a \odot \ldots \odot a$ of a, written na, such that the market-value of na is more than half the market-value of Γ.

E8. The market-value of Γ is constant for all magnitudes of M.

E9. For any (numerical) value of M, $M =_e \Gamma$.

E10. Where nm = M, for any value of n, $m =_e M/n$.

14. Market-value as a Boolean algebra

A Boolean algebra is a 6-tuple [B,$\cup$,$\cap$,′,0,1], where B is a set, $\cup$ and $\cap$ are binary operations in B, ′ is a binary relation in B having B as its domain, 0 and 1 are distinct elements of B, and for all a, b, and c belonging to B the following axioms are satisfied.

1. Each operation is associative:
   $a \cup (b \cup c) = (a \cup b) \cup c$ and $a \cap (b \cap c) = (a \cap b) \cap c$.
2. Each operation is commutative: $a \cup b = b \cup a$ and $a \cap b = b \cap a$.
3. Each operation distributes over the other: $a \cup (b \cap c) = (a \cup b) \cap (a \cup c)$ and $a \cap (b \cup c) = (a \cap b) \cup (a \cap c)$.
4. For all a in B, $a \cup 0 = a$ and $a \cap 1 = a$.
5. For each a in B there exists a ′-related element a′ such that $a \cup a' = 1$ and $a \cap a' = 0$.

The analysis of sections 7 and 8 entail certain scientifically curious requirements and possibilities for the numerical representation of market-value. Expressions E8, E9 and E10 show that the market-value of money (*including all its contemporary forms*), the operational standard, is related to the primary standard in an idiosyncratic but highly structured way. Under the terms of the convention of monetary exchange, M's market-value is identically equal to Γ's, meaning that changes in M change the market-value of M's units and not the market-value of M itself. Under these relations, the market-values of the units of money are *equal parts of the given whole market-value*, that is, the market-value of Γ. Analysis also has shown that the commensurability condition can be satisfied for market-value metrication, be it a monetary or a real economy, only by using Γ, the aggregate endowment, as the primary measurement standard. This is a situation completely at odds with the physical measurement orders of mass, length and time, where, vis-à-vis the commensurability condition, there exist an infinite number of possible primary standards for metrication. Since, for these orders, the choice of standard is ultimately arbitrary, so too is the size of the unit. Therefore, these orders can be metricated on a unit ratio scale with their measurement numbers unique up to a similarity transformation. *But market-value, since for a given aggregate endowment there is only one possible **primary** standard, may, like probability, be metricated as fractional parts of the market-value of its primary standard. Such market-value numbers would be unique up to an **identity transformation**. The fact that market-value invariably has been represented on a unit scale is irrelevant to the present inquiry.*[5] *What is important is that analysis has shown that in principle those unit scale representations e_1, e_2 ... e_n can be converted to unit-less ones, e_1', e_2'... e_n' by dividing them by M, so that $e_1' + e_2' ... + e_n' = 1$.*

Quantities of money and quantities of commodities exchanged can be interpreted as *money exchange sets and commodity exchange sets*. The special sets corresponding to M and the set of all units of all commodities exchanged in period T will be termed the *money exchange space* or Γ_M and the *commodity exchange space* or Γ, respectively. This yields $P(M_\Gamma)$ and $P(\Gamma)$, the power sets of M_Γ and Γ, which, each being a set of all subsets of a given set, are Boolean algebras. Because, as shown above by E8, E9 and E10, the market-value of M_Γ is always uniquely determined by Γ such that $M_\Gamma =_e \Gamma$, the market-value of money can be uniquely represented

[5] The nature of the scale on which a quantitative order is measured may be open to variation. Length and mass, for example, although customarily measured on a ratio scale, can be measured on an interval scale or even an ordinal scale; and temperature, although usually measured on an interval scale, can be, and in science usually is, measured on a ratio scale.

as parts of *the whole market-value*, i.e. as parts of the market-value of Γ. Furthermore, since all of the elements (units of money) comprising M_Γ are interexchangeable, i.e. of equal market-value, M_Γ is a *uniform* or *equivaluable* exchange space. It follows that where,

$$M_\Gamma = \{m_1,m_2,\ldots,m_n\}$$

and a money exchange set A is formed of g money units, that e(A), the market-value of A, is g/n parts of the whole market-value e(Γ). For every commodity exchange set, monetary exchange also identifies a money exchange set of equal market-value. Thus, when M or the cardinal of M_Γ is known, it is possible to satisfy the following conditions:

D1. With every element A of $P(M_\Gamma)$ and every element A of P(Γ), it is possible to associate a non-negative number e′(A), the *absolute market-value* of A, such that $0 \leq e'(A) \leq 1$.

D2. $e'(M_\Gamma) = e(\Gamma) = 1$.

D3. If A and B are mutually exclusive subsets of M_Γ or of Γ, i.e., if $A \cap B = \varnothing$, then $e'(A \cup B) = e'(A) + e'(B)$.

D4. For every e′(A), where A is a subset of M_Γ or of Γ, there is an element e′(A′) such that $e'(A) + e'(A') = e'(M_\Gamma) = e'(\Gamma) = 1$.

Condition D1 specifies a set $E_{M\Gamma}$ or E_Γ of absolute market-value numbers for $P(M_\Gamma)$ or for P(Γ) respectively. *Conditions D1-4 determine that* $E_{M\Gamma}$ *and* E_Γ *are Boolean algebras.*

Under the Boolean hypothesis, increasing or decreasing the size of a commodity's exchange set assumes a theoretical significance which *transcends the individual commodity market.* Any change in the size of a single market exchange set means that the commodity exchange-space Γ also changes. If Γ_1 was the original exchange space and A_1 was the ath commodity's market exchange set, then, after $A_1 \odot A_2$, the new exchange space is $\Gamma_2 = \Gamma_1 \cup A_2$. *This represents a change in the standard of market-value.* Consequently, the market-values of the elements of $P(\Gamma_1)$ and $P(\Gamma_2)$ are not *strictly* comparable. The algebraic analysis of value identifies every market-value as a part of a whole market-value, and $e(A_1)$ and $e(A_1 \odot A_2)$ represent market-values which are parts of two different wholes. This attribute of being defined only relative to a particular universal set, which is *the ultimate basis of the index number problem*, is a peculiarity of the Boolean structure. This relativity property manifests itself in other Boolean fields. For example, for every set of statements there is a different statement calculus, and the probability numbers of events belonging to different event spaces are not combinable by arithmetical addition.

15. Application to two famous theoretical paradoxes

This section considers the relevance of the foregoing results to a pair of theoretical problems which have resisted solution. Both anomalies appeared when analysis began from a non-zero degree of aggregation.

a. The homogeneity problem

After the appearance of *The General Theory* (1936), efforts were made to overcome the micro/macro split that had always been the fault-line of economic analysis. These attempts centred on the integration of money into the general equilibrium model. But these efforts at synthesis revealed an antinomy that was potentially as undermining to existing economic theory as the results of the Michelson-Morley experiment had been to classical physics. The impasse centred on the so-called "homogeneity postulate". Whereas the n equations for excess demands in the commodity markets were homogeneous of degree zero in money prices, the one equation for the excess demand for money was homogeneous of degree one in money prices and the quantity of money, an apparent contradiction where the excess demand for money is taken to be identically equal to an excess supply of commodities [Patinkin, 1956; Fullbrook, 1992; 1993; 1994].

Seen through the lens of this chapter's structural analysis, the homogeneity difference in the monetarized general equilibrium model, far from being a problem, *is precisely what is predicted*. This difference arises, according to the new approach, because the money demand equation introduces a quantitative order with a different structure from that of the unit ratio scale of money prices. In other words, the monetarized model of General Equilibrium Theory brings directly into play the Boolean structure of market-value. Exactly how this introduction takes place needs examination.

When the *market-values* of quantities of money are considered at the micro level, i.e., the market-values of subsets of M_Γ, they exhibit the same structural properties as the n quantitative orders of the n commodities. In other words, if M_1, M_2, and M_3 are disjoint subsets of M_Γ – as, for example, three ten-dollar bills in one's wallet – then their market-values are combinable according to the conditions A1-5, as are also the probabilities of independent events belonging to the same event space. But when the market-value of money is considered at the *macro* level, as is the case when a change in M_Γ is entertained, then the analysis is brought up against market-value's Boolean structure, especially its universal set which acts as an upper bound, thereby imposing the degree-one homogeneity on the demand for units of money.

b. The Fisher - Becker Curio

Gary Becker [1962; 1971] showed that from the existence of budget constraints alone it follows that a *market* demand curve must slope downward, whether consumer behavior is rational or not. By beginning his analysis at the level of the market, rather than at the level of the individual, Becker shows that there exists a macro budgetary effect which entails "the basic demand relations" [Becker, 1971, p. 11]. In other words, scarcity of funds is a sufficient condition for negative sloping market demand curves, and rational consumer behavior is not a necessary condition. In fact, Becker showed that the whole of the subjective side of demand theory is superfluous when it comes to the deduction of the general inverse relation between price and quantity demanded at the market level.

Becker's result needed an explanation which would integrate it into a larger theoretical edifice, but none was forthcoming. Without this theoretical grounding, Becker's "scarcity principle" remained an anomaly and, therefore, survives today only as a curious and obscure footnote to economics, with students continuing to be taught that the downward slope of the market demand curve is due to intrasubjective factors.

But Gary Becker was not the first to point out the budget effect, that is, "the effect of a change in prices on the distribution of opportunities" [Becker, 1962, p. 6]. With a different emphasis and at a higher level of aggregation, Irving Fisher noticed and expounded on the same macro dimension of *relative* prices forty years earlier. In *The Purchasing Power of Money*, Fisher writes:

> if one commodity rises in price (without any change in the quantity of it or of other things bought and sold, and without any change in the volume of circulating medium or in the velocity of circulation), then other commodities must *fall* in price. The increased money expended for this commodity will be taken from other purchases [1920, p. 178].

Note that here Fisher is not considering the absolute level of prices, which he assumes constant, but rather relative prices and how *at the macro level* there exists an interdependency between them. Fisher realized, in a way that Becker did not, that his discovery posed a major paradox for economics [1920. p. 180]. Furthermore, because Fisher carries the analysis to a higher level of aggregation, he comes much closer than does Becker to discovering the Boolean structure of market-value. His nearness to this elementary truth becomes apparent when two terms of his foregoing passage are translated into the terminology of the present chapter. Substituting "market-value" for "exchange-value", and "market-value per unit" for Fisher's "price", and "measured market-value" for his "money expended" yields the followings statement:

> If one commodity rises in market-value per unit (without any change in the quantity of it or of other things bought and sold, and without any change in the volume of circulating

> medium or in the velocity of circulation), then other commodities must *fall* in market-value per unit. The increased measured market-value for this commodity will be taken from [the market-value of] other purchases.

Thus translated, Fisher's passage captures "the part of the whole" relation which, as for probability, is one dimension of market-value. It captures also the fact that, despite all the concrete individuality that goes into market-value's making, *the market-value of every unit of every commodity is irreducibly and fundamentally a SOCIAL relation that extends as far as does the economy in which the exchange of the unit takes place.*

What Fisher could not do was explain how the micro and macro levels of "causation" were linked. His insight, like Mendel's discoveries concerning heredity, lacked a contemporaneous means of explanation. Abstract algebra was little known, and without this set of tools *the Boolean structure* which links market-value's two levels of "causation" could not be identified.[6]

16. What now?

Here is a list of the main points dealt with in this chapter.

1. Every quantitative order has a metrical structure, i.e. a metric.
2. These metrics can be observed and described with abstract algebra.

[6] This Boolean structure, with its internal relations, is consistent with Hodgson's reconstitutive downward causation, where "it is impossible to take the parts as given and then explain the whole," because the whole to some extent shapes its parts [Hodgson 2002, p. 168].

3. Market-value is a quantitative order.
4. The metrics of quantitative orders can be absolute or relative.
5. Equilibrium Economics is founded on the premise that market-value's metric is absolute. But this premise is *a priori* based rather than *empirically* based.
6. We broke with that *a priori* tradition and observed and described the metric of real-world market-value.
7. Those observations show that the metric of market-value is relative rather than absolute.
8. Every market-value in a money economy exists only as an integral and interdependent part of an intersubjective system of other market-values.
9. Further observations show that the market-value metric is homomorphic to a Boolean algebra.
10. Together points 1 to 9 identify the missing **macro→micro link.**

What can be done with this knowledge?

The results of this chapter place economics in an extreme epistemological predicament. *Market-value is the ultimate foundation of economic theory.* A description of the quantitative order of market-value has been given which, like any empirical description, could be wrong or in need of improvement. But although the description offered here fundamentally contradicts the implicit standard assumption of what is the metric of market-value, it is not challenging another empirical description of market-value's metric, because so far as I know it is the first one that has ever been offered. *For the time being then, the choice is not between two empirically based descriptions, but rather between empiricism and apriorism.*

Given this predicament, there are several options from which economics and economists individually need to choose.

1. Pretend that this book does not exist. (In the short to intermediate run this is likely be the most popular.)
2. Acknowledge this book's existence but decide that it is better to stick with Equilibrium Economics' *apriorism*, rather than getting deeply involved with *empiricism*.
3. Begin to:
   a. apply Newton's "experimental philosophy" to show what interesting propositions can be deduced from our empirical knowledge of market-value's metric. This book's next two chapters offer a rudimentary beginning to this long-term project.
   b. integrate the numerous alternative theories pertaining to various categories of real-world events which are *inconsistent with EE* and hence are now labelled "heterodox". Most of these theories will be found to be consistent with market-value's Boolean metric and with the immediate deductions that follow from it. *These now mostly isolated theories can be theoretically integrated into a Boolean Economics with enormous explanatory reach and forming a broad and deeply structured alternative to EE.*

Chapter 4

The four laws of market-value

1. Introduction

This book is based on the belief that deductions in economics, as in physics, should be based on empirically derived premises. This ultra-short chapter is fundamentally different in its epistemological nature from the preceding chapter. It is purely deductive, but its deductions are based on Chapter 3's empirical identification of market-value's structure. These deductions have self-evident radical implications for Economics 101. *Four fundamental propositions follow immediately from our knowledge that market-value's metric is Boolean.*

In the previous chapter, in seeking to discover the metrical structure of market-value, we limited ourselves to working with the assumption that the only exchangeables were those which the money-value numbers C + I = Y as used in Keynesian economics describe. But in real economies, markets for wealth or asset exchangeables – all those objects (and they may be no more than sheets of paper or digital codes) that persist as exchangeables from one period to the next – co-exist with markets for income exchangeables. And they both use the same standards and changing units of measurement, and – *but with one important exception to be explored later* – use the same measurement process to assign money-value numbers. So, we are now going to drop the simplifying income-only assumption and include all exchangeable assets.

As before we are dealing with a period of time t, and, as with C and I, we assume that these money-value quantities describing exchangeable assets are free of multiple counting.

So, let's identify and label the basic sets of things exchanged or exchangeable in the economy's markets.

2. Notation

$\mathcal{E}$ = the set of all exchangeables,

$\mathcal{E}_{\mathcal{X}}$ = any subset of $\mathcal{E}$,

$\mathcal{E}_{\mathcal{Y}}$ = the set of all exchangeables to which Y in C + I = Y pertains, i.e., the set of all goods and services exchanged in period t,

$\mathcal{E}_{\mathcal{Y}_x}$ = any subset of $\mathcal{E}_{\mathcal{Y}}$,

$\mathcal{E}_{\mathcal{C}}$ = the subset of $\mathcal{E}$ to which C as above pertains,

$\mathcal{E}_{\mathcal{I}}$ = the subset of $\mathcal{E}$ to which I as above pertains,

$\mathcal{E}_{a}$ = the set of all exchangeable assets,

$\mathcal{E}_{a_x}$ = any subset of $\mathcal{E}_{a}$,

so that:

$$\mathcal{E}_{a} \cup \mathcal{E}_{\mathcal{Y}} = \mathcal{E}$$

the set of all exchangeables.

For each of these sets there is a number of units of money for which they are exchangeable or exchanged in markets and which this book labels "money-value". These money-values will be labelled with the subscripts but in different typeface of the subsets of $\mathcal{E}$ which they describe, so, for examples:

X stands for the money-value of $\mathcal{E}_x$,

A stands for the money-value of $\mathcal{E}_a$,

Y stands for the money-value of $\mathcal{E}_y$, and then

$$A + Y = E$$

3. Four laws

Now that we know what the metrical structure of market-value is, we can immediately deduce some determinant structural relations between measurement numbers that previously were not accessible to us. Please note that these are *not* deductions from a model or a set of assumptions, but rather deductions that follow directly from our empirical discovery of market-value's real-world structure.

Because we now know that Y and A exist *only* as subsets of E, we can, as with probability, convert Y and A from their money-value unit *scale* onto a unitless *scale*, so that if we assign 1 as the market-value of $\mathcal{E}$, then, where *the primed symbols indicate market-values on a unitless scale*, it will *always* be the case, and this is the fundamental quantitative relation that underlies the market economy, that:

Law 1: A' + Y' = E' = 1.

We will label these *measurement numbers* "*absolute-values*". We now have two types of *measurement numbers* for *market-values*:

- "*absolute-value*" = the percentage that the market-value of a set of exchangeables is of the set of all exchangeables. Like probability, absolute-value is unitless.

- "*money-value*" = the number of units of money-value that *represents* the market-value of any set of exchangeables.

Law 2: All market-values are negatively interdependent.

Now that we can convert money-value measurement numbers of market-value to absolute measurement numbers of the same, it is clear that if the *market*-value of $\mathcal{E}_a$ increases or decreases, then the *market*-value of $\mathcal{E}_y$ decreases or increases by the *same* amount and vice versa. Or more generally:

- If the market-value of $\mathcal{E}_x$ increases or decreases, then the market value of $\mathcal{E} \setminus \mathcal{E}_x$ decreases or increases by the *same* amount and vice versa.

Once we have made the conversion to the unitless scale and noted the negative interdependence between market-values, it is self-evident that:

Law 3: Market-value and distribution are the same thing.

Their identity is hidden only so long as market-values are expressed only on a unit scale. In Chapter 5 we will see how this deeper understanding of distribution leads immediately to a new set of economic indicators, "redistribution rates".

The Boolean structure of market-value means that:

Law 4: Disequilibrium is a market-economy's perpetual state.

How does this follow?

> *First premise*: Individual markets move toward equilibrium by adjusting the price and which changes the market-value of that market's exchangeable. (This proposition is a carryover from EE and is consistent with market-value's Boolean metric.)
> *Second premise*: Law 2 - All market-values are negatively interdependent.

Conclusion: therefore, a change in the price of exchangeable x will change the equilibrium price in other markets.

Or in other words, market economies, in addition to being exogenously dynamic, are also ***endogenously dynamic*** – continuous changes resulting from internal "forces" coming from as many different directions as there are markets.

Changes in price (*money*-value per unit) are how a market equalizes supply and demand, and thereby tends toward equilibrium. This is a central hypothesis of Equilibrium Economics, and this book's findings do not dispute it. But EE goes much further than this and *a priori* asserts that with all markets doing this, the whole economy will be tending toward equilibrium. But we now know, given market-value's Boolean metric, that ***a general equilibrium is impossible.*** *Every micro market-value exists only as a part of the whole market-value.* This macro dependency of micro market-values, this *macro→micro link*, means that any price change in market X will change *the market-value of the prices* (not the prices themselves) in every other market, thereby, if they were in equilibrium, dis-equilibrating them. Market-value's Boolean metric means that in the context of the real-world it is meaningless to think in terms of equilibrium beyond the realm of individual and isolated markets, that is, beyond the linear or Euclidean level of the economy.

Chapter 5
Tank money and Boolean variables

1. Introduction

There is a strange symmetry to the formalised incomprehension of the metric of market-value that has plagued economics through the centuries. On the one hand there has been the failure to perceive its *macro* algebraic structure (Chapter 3) and on the other how its existence comes to be only through *measurement operations* at the *micro* level (Chapter 2). The second failure has led to the profession's and the general public's failure to see the everyday role of politics and speculation in determining market-values and, as we now know, distribution.

To address this failure, we need to define, based on what we have learned about the metric of market-value in the preceding chapters, a few more new quantitative concepts, including indicators that will illuminate ways, now largely hidden from view, of how a given economy is functioning in historical time.

2. The general inflation rate

"Inflation" is a key term and concept for economists and for journalists reporting on economies and for politicians pushing their agendas. As used, the term refers almost exclusively to changes in the price level of consumer goods ("cost of living"), although sometimes to the "wage level" and, since the Global Financial Crisis, to changes in the price level of financial assets. But now that market-value's metric has been identified, the concept of inflation can be greatly expanded and integrated into economics' new theoretical core, and perhaps eventually the term "inflation" will be depoliticized.

Where $\mathbf{u}_n$' stands for the *absolute market-value of the money-value unit* (e.g. a dollar) at end of time period n, and where $\mathbf{E}^\circ_n$ stands for the coefficient of the denominate number **E** (i.e., the money-value of period n's ε) at end of time period n, we have:

$$\mathbf{u}_n = \mathbf{1} / \mathbf{E}^\circ_n$$

So that the *rate of change in the market-value of the monetary unit* is:

$$\mathbf{b} = (\mathbf{u}_2 / \mathbf{u}_1) - \mathbf{1}$$

This is the heretofore undefined *general* inflation rate, and which might also be named "Boolean redivision rate".

3. Redistribution rates

Some economic indicators are more relevant to the real-world than others. With the global economy rapidly bringing us to the threshold of ecological collapse, if civilization decides to try to save itself, then the primary economic indicators are going to shift from gross product to distribution of wealth, distribution of income and to the distribution between income and wealth.

For this new priority we will need *redistribution rates*. Now that we have uncovered the economy's quantitative macro dimension, redistribution rates are easily defined and readily amenable to regular statistical computation and reporting. Their use, however, will be resisted by economists owned by The One Percent.

We can use the *general inflation rate* defined above to define the rate at which the *absolute market-value* of any subset $\mathcal{E}_{\mathcal{X}}$ of $\mathcal{E}$ changes (**r**) between two points in time.

Between two periods of time, let

> $\mathbf{r_x}$ = the *market-value redistribution* rate of $\mathcal{E}_{\mathcal{X}}$, such that
>
> $$\mathbf{r_x = X_2 / X_1 - 1 - b}$$

Along with the redistribution rates of different wealth levels and different income levels, the following four redistribution rates, those for A^m, Y^m, C^m and I^m, are of special importance:

- **asset or wealth redistribution rate**

  $$\mathbf{r_A = A_2{}^m / A_1{}^m - 1 - b}$$

- **income redistribution rate**
  $$\mathbf{r_Y = Y_2^m / Y_1^m - 1 - b}$$
- **consumption redistribution rate**
  $$\mathbf{r_C = C_2^m / C_1^m - 1 - b}$$
- **investment redistribution rate**
  $$\mathbf{r_I = I_2^m / I_1^m - 1 - b}$$

4. Market manipulation

Given that a market is a system of measurement, it, like any measurement system, is open to manipulation. Historically, economics has given attention to how the market-value measurements of individual markets can be manipulated from the supply side, e.g., oligopoly and monopoly. But, excluding advertising, demand-side manipulation of market-value measurement numbers has traditionally been treated as something originating at the macro level, i.e. changes in the total money supply and government spending. This tradition is completely at odds with market-value's Boolean metric. It also blanks from view what in our time should be a primary focus of political economy.

Changes (excluding of course definitional ones) in the *general inflation rate* can take place *only through operations at the micro, i.e. the market, i.e. the measurement, level.* It is only through changes in the market-value numbers of individual exchangeables that a change in the *general inflation rate* subsequently comes about. Changes in the quantity of money[1] exchanged can be aggregated, but *those changes come into being only when the new money is used in the economy's micro measurement operations.*

Therefore, any real-world decision to change the quantity of money exchanged is also a decision to change the distribution of income and wealth. In which markets (e.g. investment goods or assets), one should ask, will the new money enter market exchanges, i.e. measurement operations? The positive effect of new-money's entry into market X on X's money-value may lead to positive effects on the money-value of other exchangeables, but of a proportionately lower magnitude, *thereby resulting in a lowering of the absolute market-value of non-X.*

Although inflation and increases in the money supply are macro realities, they can come into being only at the micro level. Governments can decide to increase the nation's money supply, but when it comes to doing it, the government must make decisions, either directly or by delegating to others the power to make them, as to which individual markets will be targeted with the new money. Similarly, banks extend credit for use not in markets in general but rather for particular markets. These operations rather than being analogous to dispersions by helicopters are analogous to targeted insertions by tanks. In other words, in the real-world new money is always *tank money*, never helicopter money.

Markets successfully targeted with new money will experience an increase in the market-value of their set of exchangeables, and which, because of the Boolean structure of market-value, constitutes a redistribution of income and

---

[1] Here as everywhere in this book "money" includes money in all its forms.

wealth. But it is not just that some people will be losers and others winners, it is also that, depending on the *politics*, a few or even a tiny few may be winners to an extraordinary degree and with everyone else a loser.

5. Asset markets and financialization

This brings us to a point alluded to in Chapter Four. There is a fundamental difference between how market-values are assigned to goods and services and how they are assigned to assets. With the former, market-values are assigned only to those units of each category that are actually exchanged. The market-values of the unsold box of strawberries and a week of unemployment are zero. But not so with assets. The market-values of your house and of Bill Gates' portfolio exist whether sold or not.

This means that the quantity of new money needed to increase to the market-value of wealth by a given amount is a small fraction of the quantity needed to increase the market-value of income by the same amount. A good name is needed for this radical structural disparity in the market-value system, but I have not been able to think of one. It is this categorical disparity in the way that market-values are assigned that makes *financialization* possible, and which in addition to market-value's Boolean metric always makes *political economy*, secretly or otherwise, the dominant form of applied economics.

Coda

One way of looking at the history of economics is as an endless war between micro and macro. Of course, ideological and remunerative motivations have played prominent roles in amplifying this war. But these non-epistemological forces have remained so powerful in our discipline only because a general explanation of micro and macro economic phenomena that is neither micro-reductionist nor macro-reductionist has been missing. Without that link at the elementary level, economists, even ones of great intellectual integrity, must in most cases commit themselves, even before they begin to build a career, to one of the two forms of reductionism. Keynes, groomed by Marshall, was no exception. But then he began, perhaps because he hung out with non-economists, to let his mind wander, leading to those "mare's nests", as Samuelson called them, and which have been the primary inspiration for the work that lies behind this book.

References

Akerlof, George A. (2001) "Behavioral Macroeconomics and Macroeonomic Behavior", Sveriges Riksbank Prize Lecture, December 8.

Arrow, Kenneth J. and Gerard Debreu (1983 [1954]) "Existence of an Equilibrium for a Competitive Economy", *Collected Papers of Kenneth J. Arrow*, vol. 2. Cambridge, Massachusetts: Belknap, pp. 58-91.

Becker, Gary S. (1962) "Irrational Behavior and Economic Theory", *The Journal of Political Economy*,Vol. LXX, No. 1, February, pp. 1-13.

Becker, Gary S. (1971) *Economic Theory*, New York: Knopf.

Campbell, Norman R. (1928) *An Account of the Principles of Measurement and Calculation*, London: Longman's, Green & Co.

Carnap, Rudolf (1966) *Philosophical Foundations of Physics: An Introduction to the Philosophy of Science*, New York: Basic Books.

Clower, R. W. (1965) "The Keynesian Counter-revolution: a theoretical appraisal", *The Theory of Interest Rates*, F. H. Hahn and F. Brechling (eds.) London: Macmillan.

Clower, R. W. (1967) "A Reconsideration of the Microfoundations of Monetary Theory", *The Economic Journal*, vol. 6, pp. 1-9.

Debreu, Gérard (1974) "Excess-demand functions", *Journal of Mathematical Economics*, **1**: 15–21.

Debreu, Gérard (1977) *Theory of Value: An Axiomatic Analysis of Economic Equilibrium*, Yale University Press.

Debreu, Gérard (1986) "Theoretic models: mathematical form and economic content", *Econometrica*, November, pp. 1259–1270.

Duhem, Pierre (1977) *The Aim and Structure of Physical Theory*, (1905), New York: Atheneum.

Dupuy, Jean-Pierre (1989) "Convention et Common knowledge", *Revue économique*, No. 2, mars., pp.361-400.

Einstein, Albert (1952) "On the Electrodynamics of Moving Bodies", *The Principle of Relativity*, New York: Dover.

Ellis, Brian (1966) *Basic Concepts of Measurement*, Cambridge: Cambridge University Press.

Feather, Norman (1959) *Mass, Length and Time*, Edinburgh: Edinburgh University Press.

Fisher, Irving (1920) *The Purchasing Power of Money: Its determination and Relation to Credit, Interest and Crises*, New York: Macmillan.

Fullbrook, Edward (1992) "Some Surprises (Mostly Good) Regarding the Representation of Value", *Atlantic Economic Society Best Papers Proceedings*, Vol. 2, No. 2, July, pp. 13-17.

Fullbrook, Edward (1993) "Logic and Abstract Units of Account", *Atlantic Economic Society Best Papers Proceedings*, Vol. 3, No, 2, July, pp. 2-6.

Fullbrook, Edward (1994a) "Rabbit or Duck: An Introduction to Measurement Economics", presented to the American Economic Association, Boston, Mass., January.

Fullbrook, Edward (1994b) "Nominal Versus Real Values: A Nominal Distinction", *Atlantic Economic Society Best Papers Proceedings*, Vol. 4, No. 1, January, pp. 11-18. Reprinted in *Archives of Economic History*, Vol. V, No. 2, 1994, pp. 165-174.

Fullbrook, Edward (1996a) "Consumer Metaphysics: The Neoclassicalists Versus The Intersubjectivists", *Archives of Economic History*, Vol. VII, No. 1 January.

Fullbrook, Edward (1996b) "The Metaphysics of Consumer Desire and the French Intersubjectivists", *International Advances In Economic Research* Vol. 2, No. 3, August.

Fullbrook, Edward (2002) "An Intersubjective Theory of Value", in *Intersubjectivity in Economics: Agents and Structures*, editor Edward Fullbrook. London and New York: Routledge, pp. 273-299. ISBN 0-415 26697-1 (hbk), ISBN 0-415-26698-X (pbk).

Garvin, Alexander (1992) "Multidimensional Structures", *Atlantic Economic Journal*, Vol. 20, No. 2, June, pp. 30-42.

Gombrich, E.H. (1977) *Art and Illusion: A Study in the Psychology of Pictorial Representation*, Oxford: Phaidon Press, 5th edition.

Hempel, Carl G. (1952) *Fundamentals of Concept Formation in Empirical Science*, Chicago: University of Chicago.

Hicks, J. R. (1946) *Value and Capital*, Oxford: Clarendon Press.

Hodgson, Geoffrey M. (2002) "Reconstitutive downward causation: Social structure and the development of individual agency", in *Intersubjectivity in Economics: Agents and Structures*, editor Edward Fullbrook. London and New York: Routledge, pp. 159-180.

Krantz, D. H., et al. (1971) *Foundations of Measurement*, vol. 1, Cambridge, Mass.: Massachusetts Institute of Technology.

Keen, Steve and Standish, Russell (2010) "Debunking the theory of the firm – chronology", *Real-World Economics Review*, issue no. 53, pp. 56-94.

Lawson, Tony (1997) *Economics and Reality*, London: Routledge.

Leijonhufvud, Axel (1968) *On Keynesian Economics and the Economics of Keynes*, London: Oxford University Press.

Leontief, Wassily (1983) "Forward" in *Why economics is not yet a Science*, ed. Alfred S. Eichner, London: Macmillan.

Levy, Thierry (1991) *Conventions et foundements de l'échange marchand et de la monnaie*, Paris: Paris-IX-Dauphine University.

Levy, Thierry (1994) "Measurement Economics, Value Theory and the Social Function of Money", *Atlantic Economic Society Best Paper Proceedings*, Vol. 4, No. 2, July, pp. 11-18.

Mantel, R. (1974) "On the characterization of aggregate excess-demand", *Journal of Economic Theory*, **7**: pp. 348-353.

Marshall, Alfred (1920) *Principles of Economics*, 8th ed., London: Macmillan.

Menger, Karl (1959) "Mensuration and Other Mathematical Connections of Observable Material", pp. 104-111, *Measurement: Definitions and Theories*, C. W. Churchman and P Ratoosh, eds. London: Chapman & Hall.

Mill, John Stuart (1984) *Principles of Political Economy, with some of their applications to social philosophy*, London.

Montgomery, S. R (1966) *Second Law of Dynamics*, Oxford: Pergamon Press.

Orléan, André (1990) "Le role des influences interpersonnelles dans la formation des cours boursieers", *Revue économique*, No. 5, septembre.

Orléan, André (1992) "Contagion des opinions et founctionnement des marchés financiers", *Revue économique*, No. 4, julliet, pp. 685-698.

Orléan, André (1998) "La monnaie autoréférentielle: réflexions sur les évolutions monétaries contemporaines", *La Monnaie Souveraine*, eds. Michel Aglietta and André Orléan, Paris: Editions Odile Jacob.

Patinkin, Don (1965) *Money Interest and Prices: An Integration of Monetary and Value Theory*, 2nd. Edit1017. "The Value of Money", *The Quarterly Journal of Economics*, Vol. XXXII, Nov. pp. 38-65.

Ricardo, David (1971) *On the Principles of Political Economy*, Middlesex: Penguin.

Russell, Bertrand (1937) *The Principles of Mathematics*, 2nd edition, London.

Samuelson, Paul (2014) *Paul Samuelson on the History of Economic Analysis: Selected Essays*, Cambridge University Press, pp. 400-401.

Shackle, G. L. S. (1949) *Expectations in Economics*. Gibson Press.

Sonnenschein, H. (1972) "Market excess-demand functions" Econometrica. 40 (3), pp. 549-563

Sonnenschein, H. (1973) "Do Walras' identity and continuity characterize the class of community excess-demand functions? " *Journal of Economic Theory*. 6, pp. 345–354.

Sraffa, Piero (1960) *Production of Commodities by Means of Commodities: Prelude to a Critique of Economic Theory*. Cambridge University Press.

Walras, Léon (1954) *Elements of Pure Economics: or The Theory of Social Wealth*, trans. William Jaffè. London: George Allen & Unwin.

Appendix 1
Logic and abstract units of account[1]

1. Introduction

Economic reasoning sometimes finds it convenient to assume the possibility of an equiproportionate change in the prices of all goods, *including the medium of exchange*. Occasionally, as in work on money illusion and in some modern formulations of general equilibrium, the assumption of this kind of price vector plays a strategic role. [Patinkin, 1965; Arrow and Hahn, 1971] An equiproportionate change in all prices, however, cannot be expressed in money prices, since money's price in terms of itself is a constant. When money is the nth good *and the unit of account*, an increasing of the currency total by a factor x will yield the price vector, (x P_1, ..., xP_{n-1}, P_n), not the equiproportionately changed one of (xP_1,...,xP_n). To overcome this logical impasse, theorists often introduce the concept of an "abstract" or "fictional" unit of account that then permits the definition of a new set of prices, called "accounting prices". Supposedly, prices expressed in an abstract unit differ from money prices in

---

[1] Originally published: Edward Fullbrook, "Logic and Abstract Units of Account", *Atlantic Economic Society Best Papers Proceedings*, Vol. 3, No, 2, July 1993, pp. 2-6.

some qualitative way that turns the equiproportionately changed price vector into a logical possibility. But is there really any formal difference between money and accounting prices? And does using an abstract unit of account really make an equiproportionate change in all prices, including money's, logically possible? This paper seeks to answer these questions.

2. Background

A familiarity with measurement theory invites the raising of these awkward questions. Measurement theory describes the formal structure of measuring operations and their associated quantitative orders, and, by so doing, serves the utilitarian end of testing constituent concepts for logical consistency. [Ellis, 1966; Garvin, 1992; Krantz, 1971] This small but important body of knowledge is uniquely relevant to economics, whose subject matter is often a measurement phenomenon. Garvin [1992], for example, has shown this to be the case for inflation.

Measurement analysis begins with the simple truth that the units of a quantitative order cannot be defined out of the blue. Instead, one must make reference, direct or indirect, to some object or process which fulfils two conditions. Firstly, the object must possess the property that is to be quantified. For example, attempts to define a unit of mass based on the square root of two or on Beethoven's Fifth Symphony will fail, because these objects lack the property of mass. Secondly, the object used to define the unit must be one that can be brought into operational relation with at least one of the objects to which the unit is to be applied. For example, someone equipped only with a balance scales, could not define from scratch a unit of mass using the moon as their standard, because they could not place it on their scales. *Only an operationally suitable object permits the definition of an initial unit.* But once this unit is defined, additional units, as large or as small as desired, can be created merely by defining them as multiples or fractional parts of the operationally defined unit. These new units of mass might be called "abstract" or "fictional", because they refer only indirectly to objects that have been weighed. Calling such units "abstract", however, does nothing to remove their definitional dependence on a unit that was defined operationally.

How then does economics cope with these logical requirements and limitations? Mainly, it appears, *by remaining unaware of them.* Although an exception will be considered shortly, economics lacks serious attempts to explain the mechanics of abstract or fictional units of account. Instead, rather like folk medicine, it is taken on faith that abstract units of account and accounting prices have the special powers that tradition attributes to them. A critical look at this rather simple matter is overdue.[2]

3. Methods

Two points must be examined. What methods exist for expressing prices in an abstract unit, that is, one that does not "coincide" with any of the goods exchanged? And do any of these methods yield a unit that permits the prices of all goods, including money, to change equiproportionately?

[2] To the apparently increasing number of economists who see economics as infected with a kind of intellectual bad faith, this background assessment may appear naive and unduly generous. Bechtold, for example, has argued forcefully that economics deploys its concepts and procedures as "techniques of *rhetoric*" and "tools of persuasion" rather than as means of scientific inquiry [Bechtold, 1992, p.8, p.11].

As with units of mass, defining a unit of account magically is not a possibility. Reference must be made, even if only indirectly, to some object possessed of the relevant property and that can be brought into operational relation with one or more of the objects to be measured. For a unit of account, this means that the object must have the property of value in exchange *and* must exchange for at least one of the goods in the economy under consideration. A unit of account's definition can avoid making a *direct* reference to one of the goods exchanged only by specifying the new unit as a fraction or multiple of a unit of account already defined. This prior unit also may have been defined "abstractly", but the regress has to have begun with a unit of account defined not by wizardry, but by direct reference to one or more of the economy's goods. *Thus, all abstract units of account are based ultimately on non-abstract units of account. Moreover, when using an abstract unit, the price of the good from which the definitional regress begins is, by logical necessity, fixed.* A more formal look at these relations is in order.

An object possessed of the property P to be quantified is chosen as a "standard". A unit of P is then defined to be equal to or some arbitrary fraction or multiple of the P magnitude of the standard under stipulated conditions. An obvious logical consequence of this definitional procedure is that in terms of any P-unit, and no matter what numerical coefficient appears in the definiens of its definition, the P-number of the standard is fixed. Furthermore, by the same logic this constancy holds for any unit u' that is part of a definitional regress as in the following:

> u' $=_{df.}$ ru, where r is a positive number and u is a previously defined P-unit.

In other words, for any P-unit such as u' defined in terms of another P-unit there is only one logically possible P-number for the standard from which the definitional regress begins.

If the abstract unit is defined, directly or indirectly, as x times the value of the nth good, then the accounting price of the nth good is definitionally set at 1/x abstract units of account. It follows that under accounting prices, the price of the nth good is no less a constant than when prices are quoted directly in terms of that good. Thus, contrary to traditional belief, using an abstract unit does nothing to eliminate the problem of there being in the all-inclusive price vector one good whose price never changes. Even with the use of an abstract or fictional unit of account, the notion of an equiproportionate change in the prices of all goods, including – if there is one – the medium of exchange, remains a logical impossibility. *Thus, accounting prices have the same limitations as money prices.*

4. Patinkin's explanation

An exception to the general rule of taking the attributed powers of abstract units and accounting prices on faith is found in the work of Don Patinkin. In his celebrated study, *Money, Interest, and Prices*, he attempts to explain the notion of an abstract unit of account and to show that, when one is used to express prices, a line of reasoning becomes possible that is not when using money prices. Patinkin introduces the concept of an abstract unit of account as follows:

> . . . [it] serves only for purposes of computation and record keeping. This unit has no physical existence; that is it does not coincide with any

> of the goods which exist in the economy. Examples of such money in various societies are well known. Perhaps the most familiar is the guinea in present-day England [Patinkin, 1965, p. 15].

Patinkin's explanation never reaches the crux of the matter. Although he cites an example of an abstract unit of account and says that such units are *not* defined by their coincidence with one of the goods in the economy, he says nothing about how an abstract of unit of account *is* defined. His attempted explanation leaves completely unspecified the terms by which such a unit may come to exist.

On this inadequate foundation Patinkin proceeds to try to show that there is a qualitative difference between accounting prices and money prices. In the following passage Patinkin distinguishes between the terms "goods", which includes money, and "commodities" which does not.

> It should be emphasized that paper money, like any other good, also has an accounting price. Thus, for example, the accounting price of the paper sterling pound is 20/21 guineas. Paper money also has a money price; but, unlike its accounting price, this, by definition, is always unity. Thus one can conceive of a change in the *accounting* prices of all *goods*. One also can conceive of a change in the *money* prices of all *commodities*. But it is a contradiction in terms to conceive of change in the *money* prices of all goods [Patinkin, p. 16].

Instead of writing "the money price of the guinea is 21/20 paper sterling pounds", Patinkin has written that the guinea price of the pound is 20/21 guineas. Expressing the numerical relation between these two units in this manner, although admissible, does nothing to alter the definitional dependence of the guinea on the paper sterling pound. It is an empirical fact that the guinea is defined in terms of the pound, not the pound that is defined in terms of the guinea. Moreover, it is the fact that the guinea "does not coincide with any of the goods which exist in the economy" that determines the order of the definitional dependency between these two units of account. As shown above, this order of dependency means that the accounting price of the good used indirectly to define the abstract unit of account depends entirely on the definition of that unit. The coefficient of the accounting price of the good serving indirectly in the definition of the abstract unit is the reciprocal of the factor of proportionality appearing in that unit's definition. Although an infinite number of different abstract units of account may be defined on the basis of any good by changing the factor of proportionality appearing in the definition, in terms of each such unit of account defined, there is only one possible price of the good that serves indirectly in the definition of the abstract unit. Therefore, given an abstract accounting unit, one cannot conceive of a change in the accounting prices of all goods. Instead, one can conceive of a change in the accounting prices of all goods but one, the exception being the good used indirectly to define the abstract unit of account. In Patinkin's example this good is the pound sterling. Thus, just as "it is a contradiction in terms to conceive of a change in the *money* prices of all goods", so it is also a contradiction to conceive of a change in the accounting prices of all goods. With respect to the logical possibility of changing the prices of all goods, there is no difference between abstract and non-abstract units of account.

The foregoing analysis assumes that the same abstract unit continues to be used as the unit in which accounting prices are expressed. If, on the other hand, a different abstract unit is adopted as the one in which accounting prices are expressed, then obviously *all* of the accounting prices change, just as all of a set of length numbers would change if the unit of length in which they are expressed were changed. But even if we supposed that by a "change in . . . prices" Patinkin really meant "a change in the abstract unit", his argument, and others like it, could not be rescued, because a change in the money unit would have a corresponding effect on money prices. Changing the unit in which *money* prices are expressed also would change the prices of all goods, including the prices of all units of money exchanged. So, either way Patinkin's words are interpreted, there is no qualitative difference between accounting and money prices.

5. Beyond the impasse

In a recent paper it has been shown that, as a quantitative order, exchange-value, like probability, has the algebraic structure of a Boolean algebra [Fullbrook, 1992]. This result was demonstrated both for a real economy and a monetary one. For the former, analysis shows that when using one of the goods as the numeraire it is logically impossible to represent more than half the aggregate endowment's exchange-value. The whole exchange-value of the aggregate endowment can be represented if and only if that endowment itself is adopted as the standard of exchange-value. By so doing, exchange-values can be "expressed as parts of the exchange-value of the aggregate endowment, and thus as fractional parts of a whole, in the same way that probabilities are conceived and expressed as fractional parts of a certainty" [Fullbrook, 1992, p. 15]. It also was shown that it is precisely this system under which token money works. The convention of monetary exchange defines token money's exchange-value by reference to the exchange-value of the aggregate endowment, each unit having an equal fractional part of the aggregate endowment's value. Just as the guinea is an "abstract" or "fictional" unit of account relative to the pound, so too is a unit of token money relative to the aggregate endowment. When the number of units of money exchanged for the aggregate endowment changes, the size of the monetary unit of account changes in the same way that the size of an abstract unit of account changes when the factor of proportionality changes in its definition.

These results will not rescue the notion of an equi-proportionate change in all prices, including that of money. They do, however, point to a different and mathematically more powerful set of symmetries, which for the next generation of mathematical economists could prove even more favourable to formal theoretical development than the ill-founded symmetry analyzed in this paper. When the aggregate endowment's exchange-value is adopted as the unit of account, it becomes possible to speak of the price of money without introducing a numeraire, without appealing to an index number and without falling into a definitional regress. Furthermore, it becomes possible to describe without logical contradiction a state of affairs resembling the one with which this paper began and for which the notion of an abstract unit of account was found lacking:

> A decrease (increase) in the *aggregate endowment price* of money may result in an equiproportionate increase (decrease) of the same proportion in the money prices of all commodities.

But the real benefit to be gained by theorizing with the aggregate endowment as the standard for the unit of account is that it brings into play the Boolean structure of exchange-value with all its attendant mathematical felicities. The weighted average, for example, of any change in the "absolute" or aggregate endowment prices of all commodities will always *sum to zero*. It does not seem improbable that, when these Boolean structures are incorporated into formal analysis, some of economics' standard theorems will prove amenable to both simplification and extension.

6. Conclusions and summary

By tradition, the notion of an equiproportionate change in the prices of all goods, including the medium of exchange, has been accepted as logically possible. The concept of an abstract or fictional unit of account generates a set of "accounting" prices that supposedly overcomes the difficulty encountered with numeraire and money prices, namely that the price of one of the goods is fixed. This study, by drawing on the most basic premises of measurement theory, has shown that it is logically impossible to define an abstract unit of account without fixing the price of one of the economy's goods. In consequence, accounting prices have the same limitations as money prices, and an equiproportionate change in the prices of all goods, including the medium of exchange, is a logical impossibility. A leading economist's case for the established beliefs regarding the powers of accounting prices was examined and disproved in terms of the foregoing arguments. Finally, it was argued that, if, for theoretical work, the value of the aggregate endowment was adopted as the unit of account, this would bring into play *the unusual algebraic structure of exchange-value.*

References

Arrow, K. J. and F. H. Hahn (1971) *General Competitive Analysis*, Edinburgh: Oliver & Boyd.

Bechtold, Brigitte H. (1992) "Economic Proofs as Rhetoric", *Atlantic Economic Society Best Paper Proceedings*, Vol. 2, No. 2, July, pp. 8-12.

Ellis, Brian (1966) *Basic Concepts of Measurement*, Cambridge: Cambridge University Press.

Fullbrook, Edward (1992) "Some Surprises (Mostly Good) Regarding the Representation of Value", *Atlantic Economic Society Best Paper Proceedings*, Vol. 2, No. 2, July, pp. 13-17.

Fullbrook, Edward (unpublished) *The Algebraic Structure of Exchange-value.*

Garvin, Alexander (1992) "Multidimensional Commodity Structures", *Atlantic Economic Journal*, Vol. 20, No. 2, June, pp. 30-42.

Krantz, D.H. et al. (1971) *Foundations of Measurement, vol. 1*, Cambridge, Mass.: Massachusetts Institute of Technology.

Patinkin, Don (1965) *Money Interest and Prices: An Integration of Monetary and Value Theory*, 2nd edition, New York: Harper & Row.

Appendix 2

Some surprises (mostly good) regarding the representation of value[1]

1. Introduction

This short paper is about numerical representation of market-value. Six aspects of this subject will be briefly considered. First, this being an unusual topic, I feel obliged to place it in perspective with regards to science in general and economics in particular. Second, I will explain the technical matters at issue. Third, the adequacy of the representation of value with a numeraire will be examined. Fourth, an alternative system of representing market-value in a "real" economy will be offered. Fifth, in light of the above, I will consider the algebraic structure of market-value. And finally, I will raise some questions about market-value representation in a monetary economy.

---

[1] Originally published as: Edward Fullbrook, "Some Surprises (Mostly Good) Regarding the Representation of Value", *Atlantic Economic Society Best Papers Proceedings*, Vol. 2, No. 2, July 1992, pp. 13-17.

2. Perspective

Through the ages certain empirical properties, such as length, temperature and probability, have been found to have structures that are formally analogous to various numerical systems. In consequence, these properties may be expressed numerically. These representations take many forms, each depending on the type of numerical system with which the analogy or homomorphism holds. In the physical sciences these representational systems are regarded as the most fundamental of all laws, and only occasionally, with profound consequences, is one found to be false. The most famous such case was the discovery that the velocity of light is a natural upper bound to velocities, and that therefore, the representational system of classical physics, which treated any velocity as theoretically possible and expressible, was erroneous [Hempel, 1952: Krantz, 1971].

Economics is distinguished from other social sciences in that most things in its domain are characterized by a non-physical property that, like mass, length and time, is representable on a ratio scale. This attribute is variously called "value", "market-value", "exchange-value" and "money-value". Yet despite this property's overwhelming importance to economics, very little seems to be known about it. I would be surprised if any of you are familiar with its formal characteristics, in the way a physicist, say, is familiar with those of physical magnitudes.

This disparity is easily explained. Among quantitative orders in science, market-value is a curiosity, because *its principal system of representation, i.e. monetary exchange, instead of being a construct and operation of our science, is part of its object of inquiry.* Since we have had neither to invent nor apply this system of representing market-value, we have not needed to begin by discovering market-value's structural properties. Even so, given market-value's starring role in economics, it would have been prudent to have investigated its formal structure before now. But there is one theoretically prominent situation where economics has devised its own system of representing market-value, which is the case of an imaginary economy without money. As an example, on the one hand, of how little we have known about the structure of market-value, and, on the other, of the prizes that are to be won by overcoming this deficiency, I would like to consider briefly the representation of market-value in a "real" economy.

3. The technical issues

First the basic technical issues must be stated. These are relatively simple. Representational systems may be classified by how unique or determinate is the number assigned to express the property. This method of classification is highly significant, because an increase in the determinateness of a science's system of representing a property usually *leads to a deepening of that science's theoretical structure.* The formal principle of the classification is that the *smaller* the range of mathematical transformations which preserve the homomorphism, i.e. the analogy between the empirical and numerical structures, the more unique is the representation of the property. If the system's number assignments involve no arbitrariness, as in the case of probability numbers, then the representation of the property is unique up to the identity transformation. If choice of a unit is the system's only arbitrary element, as with mass and length numbers, then the representation is on a ratio scale and unique up to a similarity transformation [Ellis, 1966; Suppes, 1959].

Creation of a ratio scale requires the satisfaction of various conditions, foremost of which is that a unit of the property must be defined on the basis of a standard. This is done by designating an object, or in some cases a process, which satisfies, among others, the following conditions:

1. That the object is characterized by the property,
2. That conditions can be specified which make that object's magnitude of the property determinate,
3. That duplicates of the standard can be combined in an operation that is formally analogous to arithmetic addition, and
4. That by subdividing and combining enough copies of the standard it is possible, in principle, to make it commensurable with every object in the domain.

Failure to satisfy the last condition means that the system cannot represent the property across the whole of its domain. In such cases the system of representation is said to define only a partial scale.

4. Representation of market-value with a numeraire

Money prices and numeraire prices are examples of ratio scale representations of a property on a domain of objects. The domain is the power set of a set of commodities, *and frequently this set is presumed to be the aggregate endowment of all goods.* For generations it has been universally agreed that it is possible, in principle, to use a numeraire to represent market-value across the whole of the aggregate endowment. Nevertheless, let us examine this proposition.

Physical objects only have weight within a gravitational field; likewise they can only have market-value within the context of a market. The magnitude of on object's weight depends on the particulars of the gravitational field; likewise the magnitude of its market-value, if it has one, depends on the particular conditions of the market. One of those market conditions is the number of units of a commodity exchanged. If only demand is given, the value of the units of a commodity are not additive, because, barring transfer paradoxes, the value of a unit of any commodity will vary inversely with the number of those units brought within the market context. Therefore, to make the market-value of a good's unit determinate so that we can conceive of it as representing a quantity of value, we first have to specify not only the conditions of demand, but also those of supply and thus also the number of units exchanged. But can we ever imagine market conditions which would make the value of a quantity of any good equal to the value of the aggregate endowment of all goods?

No, because such a notion leads immediately to self-contradiction. In order for a quantity of a single good to be equal in value to the aggregate endowment, it would have to be the only good in the endowment. In which case there would be no exchanges and our good would have no market-value. Similarly, any attempt to imagine the equilibrium market-value of a quantity of a good as being more than half the value of the aggregate endowment leads to contradiction, since it implies that the value of that good is greater than the combined value of all the units of all the goods for which it is exchanged. In principle, therefore, it is impossible ever to represent, with a standard commodity, more than half the market-value of the aggregate endowment, this being *a natural upper bound to the quantity of value that can be expressed under a numeraire system of representation.* Of course, in practice, the maximum representable value will normally be less than the theoretical maximum, since no commodity with have a total value equal to half that of the aggregate endowment. Furthermore, the effective range of the numerical representation will vary, depending on which good is chosen as the numeraire.

5. An alternative system

There remains only one possibility for the full representation of value in a real economy, and that is to use the aggregate endowment as the standard. Under such a system, market-value would be represented as proportionate parts of the whole market-value. This requires a method of subdividing the aggregated endowment's value in a manner that permits assignments to all the subsets. The subdivision can be made by using the coefficients in the exchange ratios and the cardinals of the exchange sets of the n commodities, all these numbers being factors of proportionality holding between two market-values. By using these factors one can determine what fractional part of the whole market-value is the market-value of each commodity unit. Then we have a system of representation, call it the F-system, where all arbitrary units have been eliminated and so the representations are unique up to the *identity transformation.* Under the F-system, the market-values are expressed as parts of the market-value of the aggregate endowment, and thus as fractional parts of a whole, in the same way that probabilities are conceived and expressed as fractional parts of a certainty. Familiarity with probability tells us that such a system has a very special mathematical structure: it is a Boolean algebra.

6. The algebraic structure of market-value

It is self-evident that the F-system's unitless scale can be converted to a ratio scale, since this entails merely a withholding of information. Any of the fractions of the whole market-value represented under the F-system can be given a name and adopted as an arbitrary unit into which all F-system value numbers are converted, thereby giving us market-value on a ratio scale. But what is significant is that, as I have shown, in an economy without money a full ratio scale can be defined only by first devising a Boolean representation. This shows that in a "real" economy, market-value – not just the F-system of representing it – *has the structure of a Boolean algebra.*

In a yet to be published book[2] I have approached this question of the algebraic structure of value from many angles. Here there is time only to consider the matter informally from the point of view of representation, where we are now faced with a paradox. How is the situation of a "real" economy, where a Boolean F-system is the only possible way of generating a full representation of market-value, to be reconciled with a money economy, where we find a full representation of value on a ratio scale without any known sign of a Boolean system? If value in a "real"

[2] Edward Fullbrook, *The Algebraic Structure of Exchange-value*

economy is the same kind, then the two sets of quantitative phenomena must have the same formal structure. But in that case, it must be possible in a money economy to represent market-value on an unitless scale, *and* a money economy's ratio scale representation must in some hidden way be based on a Boolean system. On the face of it both these possibilities seem unlikely, *because if they are the basic facts of monetary exchange, why have they not been discovered before?*

7. Representation with money

Perhaps economics has not asked the right questions. What I have tried to do in this paper is break free of a long-established Gestalt and look at a matter of ancient importance from a new point of view. I have abandoned the tacit premise that, unlike other quantitative orders, market-value is without a formal structure. I also, instead of taking the existence of a numeraire system of value representation for granted, have inquired how such a system might be constructed and found that it has an embarrassing limitation. But coming to terms with this error, a full and more determinate system of value representation was found and with it, embedded at the very heart of the science, a model of a powerful *algebraic structure*.

The representation of value in a money economy is even easier to take for granted, as its invention owes nothing to economics. So although the discipline has inquired tirelessly about problems of monetary exchange, it has inquired almost not at all about how exactly a money system of value representation works. Since Aristotle, it has been understood that the market-value of token money is artificial, in the sense that it results only from the convention which makes money one of the terms of every market transaction. This is to say that money is a secondary standard whose value in exchange is determined by reference to an unidentified primary standard. By systematically bringing the tokens into market juxtaposition with objects whose market-value is not artificial, the convention endows each token with the property of value in exchange. But from the point of view of the numerical representation of a property, this explanation begs a fundamental question. A question which, to my knowledge, has never been answered. What exactly is the primary standard of market-value by which the market-value of money is defined? And also, how does the convention determine what magnitude of this property each token possesses?

As with units of a commodity, we know that the market-value of the tokens varies inversely with the number of them exchanged. Therefore, the market-value of token-money must, in the first instance, be determined not with respect to the individual tokens, but rather with respect to *the total amount of tokens exchanged.* The market-value of the total quantity of money exchanged is, by definition, equal to the value of the aggregate endowment of commodities. In considering a "real" economy, it was shown that there is only one object which will suffice as a standard for defining that much value. Thus, on analysis, a money economy is found to have the same primary standard of market-value as the F-system "real" economy. And token money is seen to be a system of subdividing the value of the aggregate endowment, i.e. *the whole market-value*, into a set of equal parts, as a roulette wheel divides into a set of equal parts the certainty that the ball will come to rest.

But note that the direction of these relations is the reverse of what we are conditioned to expect with quantitative properties. Generally we think of them as micro or corpuscular, in the sense that an object's magnitude of a property, call it P, is some kind of a causal function of the P-magnitudes of its constituent parts. Mass, for example, is an additive function of micro-masses. But with market-values, as with probability, micro magnitudes depend on macro ones. Furthermore, for money this function can be specified: the market-value of the individual tokens is the market-value of the aggregate endowment divided by the quantity of money (M) times its velocity (V). Thus, given MV, a money economy's ratio scale of market-value can be converted to an absolutely unique scale merely by dividing each money price by MV. Then, as in a "real" economy, market-value will be represented by the F-system, where the market-value of the aggregate endowment is unity.

References

Aristotle (1976) *Ethics*, London: Penguin.

Ellis, Brian (1966) *Basic Concepts of Measurement*, Cambridge: Cambridge University Press.

Fullbrook, Edward (unpublished book) *The Algebraic Structure of Market-Value.*

Fullbrook, Edward (unpublished Paper) "The Representation Problem in 'Real' General Equilibrium Systems".

Hempel, Carl G. (1952) *Fundamental of Concept Formation in Empirical Science*, Chicago: University of Chicago.

Krantz, D.H. et al. (1971) *Foundations of Measurement*, vol. 1, Cambridge, Mass.: Massachusetts Institute of Technology.

Suppes, Patrick (1959) "Measurement, Empirical Meaningfulness, and Three-Valued Logic," in *Measurement: Definitions and Theories*, C. West Churchman and Philburn Ratoosh (Eds) London: Chapman and Hall Ltd.

Appendix 3

Copernicus and Newton vs Jevons and Walras

How did Isaac Newton come by the concept of equilibrium, and how did he come to build his theoretical mechanics around it? I don't know. But I can say with confidence that he did **<u>not</u>** do it in the following manner. He did not say to himself as follows.

> Now over there is a science that is extraordinarily successful and whose practitioners command more respect than those of any other discipline. It has identified certain basic structures as dominant in its empirical realm, and to be able to describe and analyze them it has invented a mathematics that is homomorphic to those real-world structures. What I am going to do is to make as needed simplifying assumptions so as to *define* elements and combinations of elements in **my** empirical realm of enquiry that are homomorphic to the mathematics and basic structures of the extraordinarily successful science. The idealized phenomena that *I thus specify*, I will declare the total legitimate domain of my new science.

What I have just described is *upside-down science*. It is the math or formalism that determines what structures are going to be attributed to the real-world, rather than real-world structures determining what mathematics, if any, are capable of describing them. Remember Newton's project of creating his mechanics, similarly Einstein's project of creating the General Theory of Relativity, was held up for some years while he (unawares of Leibnitz's creation) invented a mathematics that was homomorphic to the structures he was identifying in the real-world.

The history of modern economics could not be more different. In the late 19th century upside-down science came to rule economics and continues to dominate the discipline today. One finds in the foundation texts of neoclassical economics, namely Jevons and Walras, the doctrine of upside-down science explicitly and prescriptively spelled out.

Stanley Jevons in his Preface to the first edition (1871) *of The Theory of Political Economy* wrote:

> I have attempted to treat economy as a calculus of pleasure and pain... The theory of economy, thus treated, presents a close analogy to the science of statical mechanics, and the laws of exchange are found to resemble the laws of equilibrium of a lever as determined by the principle of virtual velocities. The nature of wealth and value is explained by the consideration of indefinitely small amounts of pleasure and pain, just as the theory of statics is made to rest upon the equality of indefinitely small amounts of energy [p. 44].

Similarly, Walras in his *Elements of Pure Economics* [1874, 1984] declared that

> the *pure theory of economics* . . . is a science which resembles the physic-mathematical sciences in every respect [the author's italics].

His two examples were "mechanics" and "hydrodynamics" p. 71. Soon Walras was so obsessed with his analogy that he began referring to economic competition as "the *mechanism* of competition" [p. 86], and when defining an "unstable equilibrium" wrote:

> This equilibrium is exactly similar to that of a suspended body of which the point of suspension lies directly beneath the centre of gravity... [p. 112].

In time Walras' delusions regarding the relation of his procedures to those of real science morphed into delusions of grandeur. In the "Preface to the Fourth Edition" he wrote:

> It took from a hundred to a hundred and fifty or two hundred years for the astronomy of Kepler to become the astronomy of Newton and Laplace . . . On the other hand, less than a century has elapsed between the publication of Adam Smith's work and the contributions of Cournot, Gossen, Jevons, and myself [p. 48].

Subsequently, with the passing of generations of economists and their increasing professionalization, the belief that markets, through their systems of prices, tend towards a beneficent condition formally analogous to mechanical equilibrium became not only a central structural hypothesis but also the incontestable *conceptual box* in which all mainline economic thinking took place. In a market economy it will always be the case that prices and quantities exchanged are the primary focus of economics. But when it comes to markets the formal training of economists renders us mostly incapable of thinking for long outside the equilibrium framework.

Economics is not the first science to become the prisoner of its imagined success. In astronomy geocentrism enjoyed a similar and much longer rein. Ptolemy's geocentric planetary system was heavily mathematized, more formally sophisticated than any other empirical or quasi-empirical pursuit. By comparison Copernicus' heliocentric system was crude and in consequence (1473–1543) long ignored. Faced with observations of the five then known planets orbiting the sun, Tycho Brahe (1546–1601) rescued geocentrism by declaring that although the planets orbit the sun, the sun still orbits the Earth. Even after Galileo (1564–1642) pointed to Jupiter and its moons as an example of a Copernican system, the formal sophistication of geocentrism and, more important, its inculcation into professional habits of thought enabled it to continue its hegemony, despite empirical evidence, into the 18th century.

Keynes

Another example of the power of professionally inculcated habits of mind to curtail creative thought is that of John Maynard Keynes. I say that as one who has long admired

Keynes' intellectual powers and integrity above all other economists. What is most amazing about *The General Theory*, after its genius, is what it fails to do [1936, 1974]. True, it introduced the idea that economic equilibrium might not always be a beneficent condition, nonetheless the whole theory, and nearly the whole book, is framed within the equilibrium conceptual straightjacket. But unlike Tycho Brahe, Keynes did not have at hand the conceptual framework needed to break with his intellectual past. I do not doubt that if Keynes had had one or more new broad conceptual tools that pertained to the understanding of markets, he would have used them in lieu of Jevon's and Walras' analogy from Newton's equilibrium.

But as we know there are places in *The General Theory*, especially Chapter 12, where Keynes steps outside his analytical framework, rather like someone stepping outdoors for a smoke and a chat, to drop informal observations about how markets really work. These include talk about the maintenance and breakdown of conventions [pp. 152–3] and "the mass psychology of a large number of ignorant individuals" interacting with "the professional investor and speculator". He also throws out the casual analogies of newspaper beauty competitions [p. 156], casinos [p. 159] and "animal spirits" [p. 161]. These analogies, one of which refers to reflexive phenomena, have in recent decades come to be much used and in the same casual way that Keynes used them. But they have not led, at least not directly, to the development of *a non-equilibrium analytical framework for markets*, one that might, like heliocentrism versus geocentrism, supplant or at least operate alongside equilibrium economics. Such a development requires a much more substantial conceptual basis.

Appendix 4
The political economy of bubbles[1,2]

Over the past thirty years in the US and the UK there have been large upward redistributions of income from the bottom 90 per cent to the top 1 per cent and especially to the top .1 per cent. These redistributions are specific to these economies rather than a general phenomenon of advanced economies. This paper argues that these redistributions have taken place because of fundamental changes, albeit informal, in the political structures of the US and the UK. Drawing on Citigroup reports and charting the interplay between Goldman Sachs and the Obama administration, the paper argues that these changes have been realised through organized, systematic, conceptualized and financially motivated subversions of the democratic process. Strategies for effecting and preserving these changes are examined. Some of the changes in law and government policy which were enabled by the new political structure and which in turn enabled the creation of the most recent financial bubble are listed. The paper concludes that it is in the interests of the new political

[1] Originally published as: Edward Fullbrook, "The political economy of bubbles", *Real-World Economics Review*, issue no. 59, 2012.
[2] Thanks to Jamie Morgan for suggestions. The usual disclaimers pertain.

order, secretly called "plutonomy" by its insiders, to have more financial bubbles in the future.

With courageous but inconsequential exceptions – Galbraith senior comes especially to mind – explicit political economy has for generations been essentially dormant, either the slave of historically eroded categories or a cover for ideological exercises. Recently Hudson, Keen, Baker, Wray, Kadri, Hillinger and others have struggled to awaken minds to political determinants which in our time often shape economies more profoundly than the idealized and purely economic ones traditionally portrayed in the classroom. In the spirit of their undertakings, briefly I am going to consider three hypotheses.

1. In recent decades there has been a significant change in the political structures of both the United States and the United Kingdom.

2. Recent occurrences of financial bubbles are causally related to these changes in the political structures of the United States and the United Kingdom.

3. Without a reversal of the changes in the political structures of the US and the UK, the cycle of financial bubbles and the crises that follow their collapse are likely to continue.

1. Upward redistributions

Over the past thirty years in both the US and the UK there have been large upward redistributions of income in which the beneficiaries have comprised a tiny per cent of the population and the losers the overwhelming majority, roughly ninety per cent. This pattern has not generally characterized other advanced economies. The following set of six graphs illustrates these facts.

From the following series of six graphs two general points may be drawn.

a. Because these income redistributions are country specific they must be due to government policies.

b. The graphs show that in the US and the UK these redistributions of income have taken place regardless of which political party was in power.

Exhibit 1: Average incomes including capital gains in United States 1950-2008

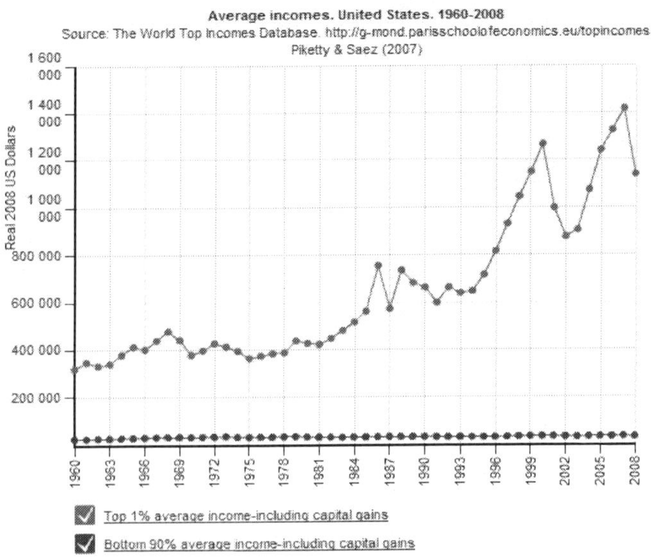

Exhibit 2: Average incomes excluding capital gains in United States 1950–2008

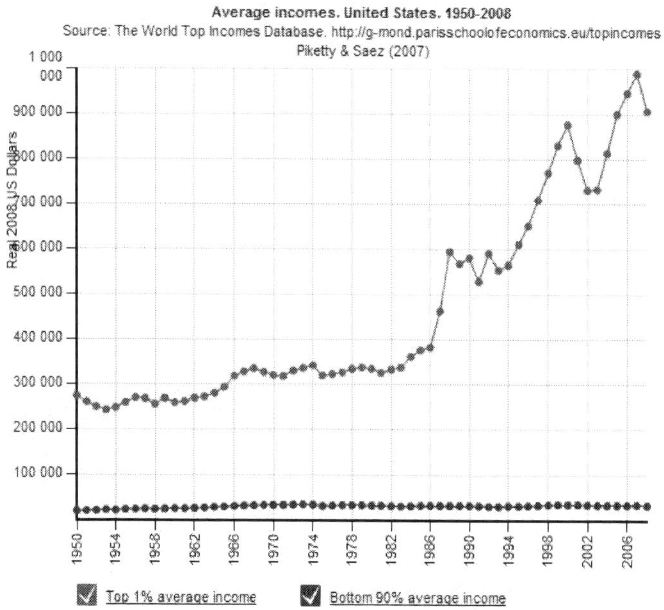

Exhibit 3: Top income shares in the United States 1960–2008

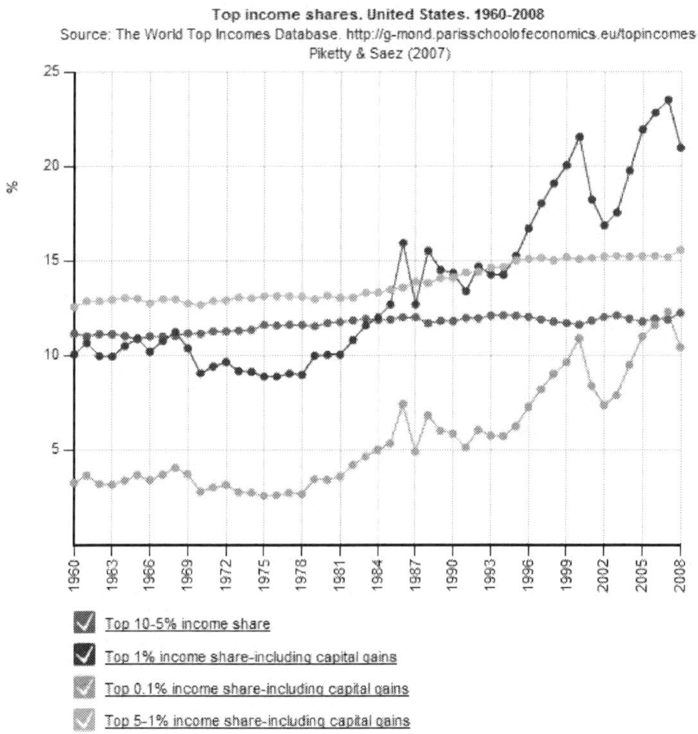

Exhibit 4: Top income shares in the United Kingdom 1960–2010

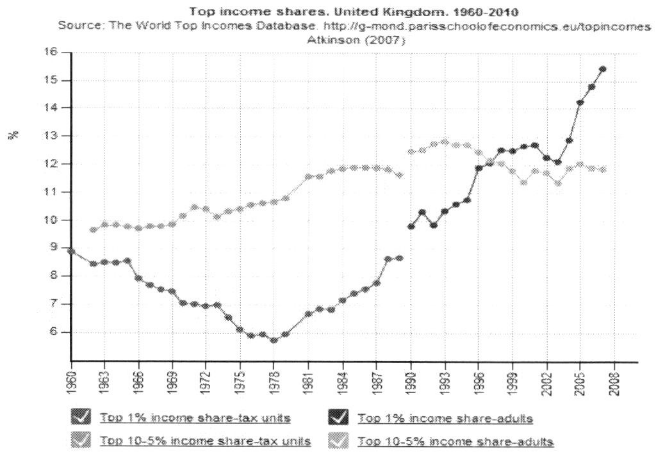

Exhibit 5: Average incomes in the United Kingdom 1960–2000

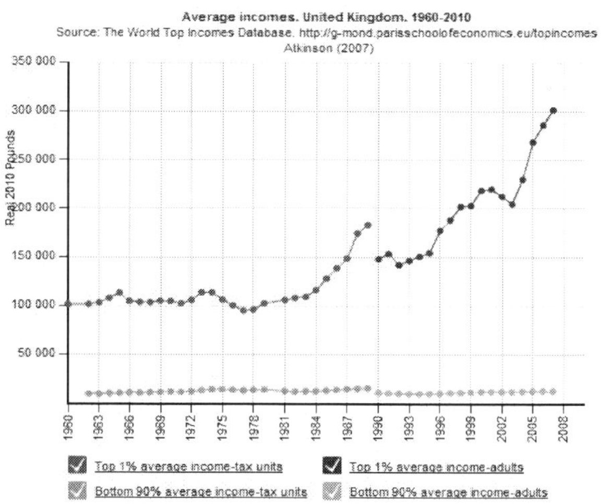

Exhibit 6: Top income shares in France, Spain and the Netherlands 1960–2006

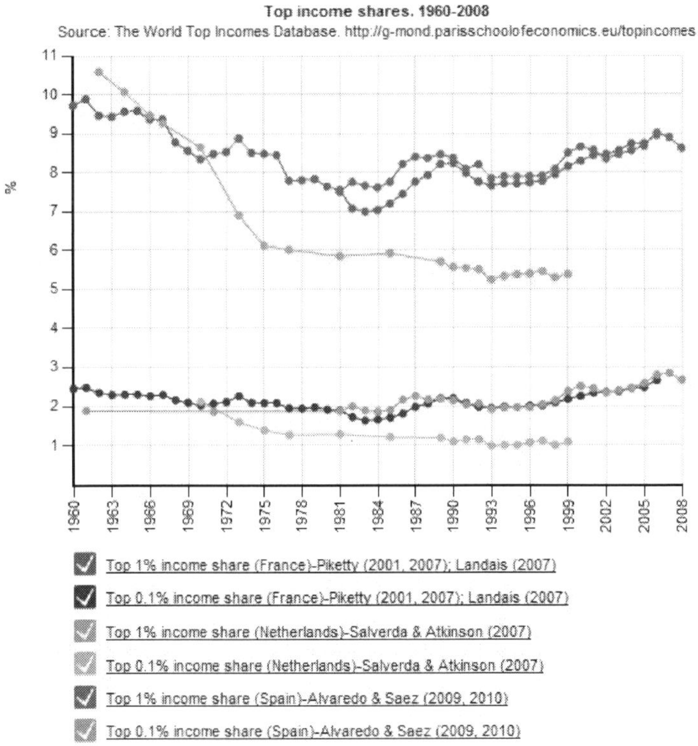

2. The new political structure: Plutonomy

The data shown in Exhibits 1–6 imply that the US and the UK have in recent decades experienced significant changes in their political structures. This is not yet a common idea. In the period focused here, roughly from 1980 to 2008, there have been no significant changes in the two countries' formal systems of government. But there is more to government than its formal structures. The same institution, for example an elected parliament or even individual political parties therein, may perform radically, systematically and intentionally differently from one historical period to the next, including with regard to the welfare of the general population.[3] The recent histories of the US and the UK are cases in point.

Excepting matters of national security, in both the UK and the US, as in most countries, the material standard of living is almost universally accepted as the primary measure of its population's welfare. Even those political parties commonly identified with the interests of the wealthy, the Conservatives in the UK and the Republicans in the US, have won their seats by convincing the majority that their policies would best serve their material interests by generating larger GDP gains that would be shared between income groups including the majority of the population.

Furthermore, in the more distant past the governments of neither of these parties have been generally associated with upward redistributions of income. And of course even in recent decades, neither the Conservatives nor the Republicans have ever openly campaigned on the promise that they would **affect an upward redistribution of income**. Indeed, in the US and the UK no political party could win elections by openly campaigning on a platform of redistributing income upward to the richest one per cent of the population. But given that governments have affected

[3] ". . . democracy in the United States has eroded; the institutions remain formally intact, but their substance has been subverted to serve the special interest over the general interest" Claude Hillinger, Economics, Vol. 4, 2010, http://www.economics-ejournal.org/economics/journalarticles/2010-23/version_1/at_download/file

these redistributions, it follows that the real agendas or platforms of the winning parties have been kept secret.

In the US and the UK either of their two major political parties could win elections **if**, unlike their opponents, **they campaigned in the usual way** but on a promise to stop or reverse the redistribution of income to the ultra-rich. Because only 1 per cent of the population benefits from these upward redistributions and the standard of living of at least 90 per cent suffer from them, it does not seem credible that the electorates would **knowingly** vote for their continuation. Furthermore the six graphs above illustrate the situation in a way that could be easily and quickly grasped by the average voter. A well-funded election campaign that focused on such graphs or the equivalent would have little difficulty getting the true significance of the election across to the majority of voters.

But currently the populations of the US and the UK appear to be nearly totally ignorant of the fact that for over thirty years their countries have been subject to the engineering of huge and extremely skewed upward redistributions of income. This central fact of contemporary political and economic existence for these countries is virtually never discussed in their general media. Nor will you find much about it in economics journals. But, as shown below, where you do find it discussed, and ever so greatly appreciated, is among the 1 per cent.

Together these points imply a change in the political structures of these countries. Why? Because if the major political parties have before them a straight-forward way of winning elections by appealing to the basic material interests of the overwhelming majority of the electorate and they repeatedly decline to do so even when it means defeat, then there must be a **non-democratic reason** that governs their decisions and their access to office. What is it?

3. The Plutonomy Reports

Unlike the 99 per cent, the 1 per cent in the US and the UK are very much aware of both the income redistributions and the new political system that make them possible. They even have a name for it: **plutonomy**. It is the term used by some of the key backers of this political ideology, political movement and concept of government, whose primary players belong to the financial sector.

The history of plutonomy's conceptual development remains clouded in secrecy. But the fact that plutonomy as a real-world political phenomenon is conceptually driven, rather than merely an historical accident, emerged to public view in 2005 when the first of three Citigroup documents prepared for its wealthiest clients were leaked.

- **"Plutonomy: Buying Luxury, Explaining Global Imbalances"** Oct. 16, 2005 (35 pages)
- **"Revisiting Plutonomy: The Rich Getting Richer"** March 5, 2006 (18 pages)
- **"The Plutonomy Symposium — Rising Tides Lifting Yachts"** Sept. 29, 2006 (64 pages)

Citigroup has gone and continues to go to great links to supress these important historical documents. Websites which post them receive threats of legal action if they are not immediately taken down, and likewise, apparently, the servers of those websites. Roughly a year and a half ago Citigroup lawyers had succeeded in removing them all. But now, using Google, it is easy to find all three documents on the Web, mostly on sites associated with The 99 Percent Movement.

Here are a few passages from the "Citigroup Plutonomy Memos" that outline, in the plutonomist's vernacular, this political ideology's key points and their view of the world. You will notice the strategic nature of these reports. It is this that makes it, from the plutonomist's viewpoint, imperative to keep the content of these historical documents from entering into mainstream discourse.

Report no. 1

> Little of this note should tally with conventional thinking. Indeed, traditional thinking is likely to have issues with most of it.
>
> The world is dividing into two blocs - the plutonomies, where economic growth is powered by and largely consumed by the wealthy few, and the rest. Plutonomies have occurred before in sixteenth century Spain, in seventeenth century Holland, the Gilded Age and the Roaring Twenties in the U.S.
>
> We project that the plutonomies (the U.S., UK, and Canada) will likely see even more income inequality, disproportionately feeding off a further rise in the profit share in their economies, capitalist-friendly governments, more technology-driven productivity, and globalization.

In a plutonomy there is no such animal as "the U.S. consumer" or "the UK consumer", or indeed the "Russian consumer". There are rich consumers, few in number, but disproportionate in the gigantic slice of income and consumption they take. There are the rest, the "non-rich", the multitudinous many, but only accounting for surprisingly small bites of the national pie.

. . . we think the plutonomy is here, is going to get stronger, its membership swelling from globalized enclaves in the emerging world, . . .

WHERE ARE THE PLUTONOMIES?

The U.S., UK, and Canada are world leaders in plutonomy... Countries and regions that are not plutonomies: Scandinavia, France, Germany, other continental Europe (except Italy), and Japan.

THE UNITED STATES PLUTONOMY

As Figure 1 shows the top 1% of households in the U.S., (about 1 million households) accounted for about 20% of overall U.S. income in 2000, slightly smaller than the share of income of the bottom 60% of households put together. That's about 1 million households compared with 60 million households, both with similar slices of the income pie!

The rich in the U.S. went from coupon-clipping, dividend-receiving rentiers to a Managerial Aristocracy indulged by their shareholders.

> **WHY THE PLUTONOMY WILL GET STRONGER WHERE IT EXISTS, PERHAPS ATTRACT NEW COUNTRIES**
> We posit that the drivers of plutonomy in the U.S. (the UK and Canada) are likely to strengthen, entrenching and buttressing plutonomy where it exists. The six drivers of the current plutonomy: 1) an ongoing technology/biotechnology revolution, 2) capitalist friendly governments and tax regimes, 3) globalization that re-arranges global supply chains with mobile well-capitalized elites and immigrants, 4) greater financial complexity and innovation, 5) the rule of law, and 6) patent protection
>
> At the heart of plutonomy, is income inequality. Societies that are willing to tolerate/endorse income inequality are willing to tolerate/endorse plutonomy.
>
> So an examination of what might disrupt Plutonomy - or worse, reverse it - falls to societal analysis: will electorates continue to endorse it, or will they end it, and why.

Report no. 2

The second report begins by identifying **three** things that have enabled the creation of plutonomies in the US, UK, Canada and Australia: "**Asset booms, a rising profit share and favourable treatment by market-friendly governments**". (emphasis added) Further on it considers:

> **What Could Go Wrong**
> . . . the rising wealth gap between the rich and poor will probably at some point lead to a political backlash. Whilst the rich are getting a greater share of the

> wealth, and the poor a lesser share, political enfrachisement remains as was – one person, one vote (in the plutonomies). At some point it is likely that labor will fight back against the rising profit share of the rich and there will be a political backlash against the rising wealth of the rich. . . . . We don't see this happening yet, though there are signs of rising political tensions. However we are keeping a close eye on developments.

Report no. 3

This is the longest of the three reports. Significantly it notes that:

> The rise of this inequality is not universal. In a number of other countries – the non-plutonomies – income inequality has remained around the levels of the mid 1970s. Egalitarianism rules. (p.9)

It singles out Japan, France, Switzerland and the Netherlands as examples and dubs them "The Egalitarian Bunch". Their deviance is then illustrated with a graph titled "The Income Share of the Top 1% Is Relatively Small Compared to Plutonomies".

Further on, after reminding the readership that "plutonomy countries" are those with "economies powered by a relatively small number of rich people" and geared to "financial wealth creation", and noting that the previous week a "Plutonomy Symposium" was held in London, "the risks to plutonomy" are, as in previous reports, considered.

> Perhaps the most immediate challenge to Plutonomy comes from the political process. Ultimately, the rise in income and wealth inequality to some extent is an **economic disenfranchisement of the masses** to the benefit of the few. However in democracies this is rarely tolerated forever. One of the key forces helping plutonomists over the last 20 years has been the rise in the profit share – the flip side of the fall in the wage share in GDP. As plutonomists or capitalists tend to be long {on} the profit share, they have benefited from trends like globalization and the productivity revolution, dis-proportionately. However, labor has, relatively speaking, lost out. We see the biggest threat to plutonomy as coming from a rise in political demands to reduce income inequality, spread the wealth more evenly, and challenge forces such as globalization which have benefited profit and wealth growth. [emphasis added]

Nonetheless:

> Our own view is that the rich are likely to keep getting even richer, and enjoy an even greater share of the wealth pie over the coming years.

These three plutonomy tracts, being windows both into the plutonomist's mind and to their strategies, contain many interesting points, but for democrats the most significant one is that **plutonomists see the subversion of democratic process as the ultimate key to their success.** If the "political enfranchisement remains" and is allowed to remain, then the "economic disenfranchisement of the masses" is only possible if they can be bamboozled into voting against their interests. It seems inevitable therefore, that plutonomists and their agents have gone to great lengths to suppress these documents.

4. Plutonomy's means to power

How does the financial industry come to control the political parties and individual politicians?

Cost of winning elections is the cost of running a plutonomy.

In the US it has long been the case that the ultra-rich, if so inclined, could buy themselves or a favourite son a seat in Congress. What has changed is that it is has become so expensive to win a seat in the House or the Senate that it no longer is generally possible to do so without the backing of The One Percent. The Open Secrets Organization reports that in the 2010 elections the winners of seats in the House of Representatives spent on average $1,439,997 and the winners for the Senate averaged $9,782,702.[4]

This, however, is just the tip of the iceberg. Between 1998-2008, according to the Wall Street Watch Organization, the financial industry spent more than 5 billion dollars on lobbying and campaign contributions. This included

> more than $1.738 billion in federal elections from 1998-2008. Primarily reflecting the balance of power over the decade, about 55

[4] http://www.opensecrets.org/bigpicture/elec_stats.php?cycle=2010

> percent went to Republicans and 45 percent to Democrats. Democrats took just more than half of the financial sector's 2008 election cycle contributions.
>
> The industry spent even more — topping $3.3 billion — on officially registered lobbyists during the same period. This total certainly underestimates by a considerable amount what the industry spent to influence policymaking. U.S. reporting rules require that lobby firms and individual lobbyists disclose how much they have been paid for lobbying activity, but lobbying activity is defined to include direct contacts with key government officials, or work in preparation for meeting with key government officials. Public relations efforts and various kinds of indirect lobbying are not covered by the reporting rules.
> [http://wallstreetwatch.org/reports/part2.pdf]

Plutonomy policy changes in the United States

Since 1980 a long series of legislative and executive changes have been made to United States government policy whose effect has been to redistribute income upwards towards the ultra-rich and to increase the concentration of wealth. These changes have taken place in approximately equal measure under Republican and Democratic administrations. Robert Weissman, in an article[5] for Alternet, describes 12 plutonomy inspired deregulatory moves. His first 5 items are as follows:

---

[5] http://theragblog.blogspot.com/2009/03/financial-meltdown-12-corrupt-deals.html

1. The repeal of Glass-Steagall

The Financial Services Modernization Act of 1999 formally repealed the Glass-Steagall Act of 1933 and related rules, which prohibited banks from offering investment, commercial banking, and insurance services. In 1998, Citigroup and Travelers Group merged on the expectation that Glass-Steagall would be repealed. Then they set out, successfully, to make it so. The subsequent result was the infusion of the investment bank speculative culture into the world of commercial banking. The 1999 repeal of Glass-Steagall helped create the conditions in which banks invested monies from checking and savings accounts into creative financial instruments such as mortgage-backed securities and credit default swaps, investment gambles that led many of the banks to ruin and rocked the financial markets in 2008.

2. Off-the-books accounting for banks

Holding assets off the balance sheet generally allows companies to avoid disclosing "toxic" or money-losing assets to investors in order to make the company appear more valuable than it is. Accounting rules - lobbied for by big banks - permitted the accounting fictions that continue to obscure banks' actual condition.

3. CFTC blocked from regulating derivatives

Financial derivatives are unregulated . . . During the Clinton administration, the Commodity Futures Trading Commission (CFTC) sought to exert regulatory

> control over financial derivatives, but the agency was quashed by opposition from Robert Rubin and Fed Chair Alan Greenspan.
>
> *4. Formal financial derivative deregulation: the Commodities Futures Modernization Act*
>
> The deregulation - or non-regulation - of financial derivatives was sealed in 2000, with the Commodities Futures Modernization Act. Its passage orchestrated by the industry-friendly Senator Phil Gramm, the Act prohibits the CFTC from regulating financial derivatives.
>
> *5. SEC removes capital limits on investment banks and the voluntary regulation regime*
>
> In 1975, the Securities and Exchange Commission (SEC) promulgated a rule requiring investment banks to maintain a debt to-net capital ratio of less than 15 to 1. In simpler terms, this limited the amount of borrowed money the investment banks could use. In 2004, however, the SEC succumbed to a push from the big investment banks - led by Goldman Sachs, and its then-chair, Henry Paulson - and authorized investment banks to develop net capital requirements based on their own risk assessment models. With this new freedom, investment banks pushed ratios to as high as 40 to 1.

President Obama is on record as favouring raising the top marginal income tax rate from its current 35% to 39.6%. The table below shows what that rate has been since the end of World War Two. The years in red were those in which a Democrat was president and those in blue a Republican. From 1953 to 1960 Dwight Eisenhower, a middle of the road Republican, was president. And for two of those years the Republican Party also controlled Congress. Yet Eisenhower chose to keep the top rate at 91%. Does that mean that Eisenhower and his Republican Congress were a million miles to the left of Obama? No, of course not. The left-right metaphor no longer pertains to the primary economic issues of the age in which we live. To use it in that context merely obfuscates. Rather than left versus right, the dividing line in today's political economies is The One Percent versus The 99 Percent. And in the US and the UK, regardless of which political party rules, it is The One Percent who are in control.

Exhibit 7: Top Marginal Income Tax Rate in the US 1946–2011

Year / Top Marginal Rate	Year Top Marginal R /ate
1946 86.45%	1979 70.00%
1947 86.45%	1980 70.00%
1948 82.13%	1981 69.13%
1949 82.13%	1982 50.00%
1950 91.00%	1983 50.00%
1951 91.00%	1984 50.00%
1952 92.00%	1985 50.00%
1953 92.00%	1986 50.00%
1954 91.00%	1987 38.50%
1955 91.00%	1988 28.00%
1956 91.00%	1989 28.00%
1957 91.00%	1990 31.00%
1958 91.00%	1991 31.00%
1959 91.00%	1992 31.00%
1960 91.00%	1993 39.60%

1961 91.00%	1994 39.60%
1962 91.00%	1995 39.60%
1963 91.00%	1996 39.60%
1964 77.00%	1997 39.60%
1965 70.00%	1998 39.60%
1966 70.00%	1999 39.60%
1967 70.00%	2000 39.60%
1968 75.25%	2001 38.60%
1969 77.00%	2002 38.60%
1970 71.75%	2003 35.00%
1971 70.00%	2004 35.00%
1972 70.00%	2005 35.00%
1973 70.00%	2006 35.00%
1974 70.00%	2007 35.00%
1975 70.00%	2008 35.00%
1976 70.00%	2009 35.00%
1977 70.00%	2010 35.00%
1978 70.00%	2011 35.00%

Revolving doors

Movements of personnel between roles in government, seen as crucial to the financial position of The One Percent, and extravagantly paid roles (formal and otherwise) in One Percent institutions are maintained. Motivation for maintaining these movements includes an appreciation of the complex dynamics of their socio-cultural contexts. One such revolving door illustrates the case.

Exhibit 8: The revolving door between Goldman Sachs and the Obama Administration

	Name	Relation to Goldman Sachs and its offshoot the Hamilton Project	Position in Obama Administration
1	Obama, Barack	Goldman Sachs employees contributed $994,795 to Obama's presidential bid.	President
2	Biden, Joe	Goldman has been a major campaign contributor to Biden.	Vice President
3	Altman, Roger	Hamilton Project Member and was Assistant Secretary of the Treasury under "Mr. Goldman Sachs", Robert Rubin.	He is "one of those power brokers with all- encompassing contacts within the Democratic Party".
4	Brainard, Lael	Associate and protégé of Robert Rubin.	United States Under Secretary of the Treasury for International Affairs.
5	Buffett, Warren	He has invested billions in Goldman Sachs.	He is one of Obama's fundraisers and economic advisers.
6	Clinton, Hillary	In 2008 she received $415,000 (inflation adjusted) from Goldman Sachs.	United States Secretary of State
7	Craig, Gregory	He left the White House to become Goldman Sach's chief lawyer in defending against its SEC suit.	He was Obama's White House Counsel.

8	Donilon, Thomas	He was a lawyer at O'Melveny and Myers representing meltdown clients including Goldman Sachs.	Deputy National Security Adviser to Barack Obama.
9	Dudley, Bill	He joined Goldman in 1986 and was partner and managing director until 2007.	Federal Reserve Bank of New York President since January 2009
10	Elmendorf, Douglas	He previously was the Director of the Hamilton Project.	He became *Obama's Director of the Congressional Budget Office* in January 2009.
11	Emanuel, Rahm	Received large contributions from Goldman Sachs as a Congressman and was on a $3,000 a month retainer from Goldman while he worked as Bill Clinton's chief fund raiser.	Obama's Chief of Staff, the very first person Obama selected to be in his administration.
12	Farrell, Diana	She worked for two years at Goldman Sachs.	Deputy Director of the National Economic Council.
13	Friedman, Stephen	He worked for much of his career with Goldman Sachs, holding numerous executive roles and still serves on the company board.	Chairman of Obama's Foreign Intelligence Advisory Board.
14	Furman, Jason	Former Director of the Hamilton Project	He was director of economic policy for the Obama Presidential Campaign.
15	Fudge, Anne	Trustee of the Brookings Institution within which the Hamilton Project is embedded	Member of Obama's budget deficit reduction committee.

16	Gallogly, Mark	He is member of the Hamilton Project's advisory council.	He is a member of President Barack Obama's President's Economic Recovery Advisory Board.
17	Geithner, Timothy	A protégé of both Henry M. Paulson Jr., a former chief executive of Goldman Sachs, and Robert Rubin, former co-chairman of Goldman Sach.	He was Obama's Secretary of the Treasury.
18	Gensler, Gary	He was a Goldman Sachs partner.	Obama's Commodity Futures Trading Commission head.
19	Greenstone Michael	Director of the Hamilton Project	He was an economic adviser position to Obama.
20	Hormats, Robert	27 years at Goldman Sachs, including as the Vice Chairman of Goldman's international arm.	The top economics official at Obama's State Department.
21	Kashkari, Neel.	Former Vice President of Goldman Sachs	He worked for Obama on TARP oversight.
22	Kornbluh, Karen	She was Deputy Chief of Staff to Robert Rubin.	Obama's Ambassador to the OECD
23	Lew, Jacob	He sits on the Brookings-Rubin funded Hamilton Project Advisory Board.	United States Deputy Secretary of State for Management and Resources.
24	Orszag, Peter	He was the founding director of Goldman Sachs' Hamilton Project	Obama's Budget Director.

25	Patterson, Mark	Former lobbyist for Goldman Sachs	Overseer of TARP bailout funds, $10 billion of which went to Goldman.
26	Rattner, Steve	A billionaire financier who sits on the Advisory Council of the Goldman funded Hamilton Project.	He oversaw the Obama Administration's rescues of General Motors and Chrysler.
27	Reischauer, Robert	He has close ties to Robert Rubin and sits on the Advisory Council of the Goldman funded Hamilton Project.	Appointed by Obama as one of the two public trustees of the Social Security and Medicare trust fund.
28	Rivlin, Alice	She is a member of the Hamilton Project board and of the board of directors of the New York Stock Exchange.	Appointed by Obama to his "deficit reduction commission".
29	Rubin, James	Son of Robert Rubin (see next entry).	Served as a headhunter for Obama.
30	Rubin, Robert	26 years at Goldman Sachs and its former co-chairman. Also former Chairman of Citigroup. Along with Goldman Sachs, he funded the Hamilton Project.	Regarded by insiders as the de facto President of the United States.
31	Sperling, Gene	In 2008 he was paid $887,727 by Goldman Sachs as a consultant.	Advisor to Obama'sTreasury Secretary Tim Geithner on financial bailouts and other matters.

32	Storch, Adam	Former Vice President of Goldman Sachs.	Obama appointed him Managing Executive of the Security and Exchange Commission's Division of Enforcement.
32	Summers, Larry	He landed a big-time job at Goldman Sachs after crashing as Harvard's President. In 2008 Goldman Sachs paid him $135,000 for a single speech.	Obama's chief economic adviser and head of the National Economic Counsel.

Source: compiled from "A List of Goldman Sachs People in the Obama Government", by fflambeau, April 27, 2010, http://my.firedoglake.com/fflambeau/2010/04/27/a-list-of-goldman-sachs-people-in-the-obama-government-names-attached-to-the-giant-squids-tentacles/

Pultonomy's strategic policy

From the foregoing cursory look at the workings of plutonomy there emerges a basic outline of its strategic policy.

- The radically skewed upward redistributions of income are kept out of the news and public discussion.
- The *primary policies* of the major political parties, i.e., those effecting and preserving the income redistributions, are kept a secret from the electorate.
- The financial cost of winning elections is kept at a level which requires the financial and media support of the One Percent, meaning that, with rare exceptions, winning candidates campaign on a platform and in a manner that does not jeopardise the upward redistribution of income.

- Office holders know that in time large financial rewards are likely to accrue to them if they serve well plutonomy's interests.
- This decisive leverage is then used
    - to control government economic policy, and
    - to control appointments to economically key government positions.

There are many ways that power operates to produce a confluence of outcomes and a broad shape to policy in terms of what is deemed possible and what is preferred. These range from simple pressure, to the broader disciplining of policy venues, networks and actors that expresses itself in institutions and organizations. All are relevant to the way Plutonomy maintains power.

Plutonomy and financial bubbles

Plutonomy's power base is of course the financial rather than the industrial sector of the economy. The US and UK economies have been financialized, meaning, among other things, that the financial sector no longer sees its primary function as servicing the financial needs of the industrial sector, in particular, the raising of funds for economic investment. Instead of being seen as one of the means of economic production, financial assets have come to be seen as ends in themselves. Under financialization fortunes are sought not through the profits of economic production, but rather through financial assets themselves. This pursuit takes three primary and interconnected forms:

1. Creation of leverage or Ponzi schemes that enable huge expansion of one's financial holdings;

2. The securitizing of debts, often in a fraudulent manner;
3. Profiting from changes in the values of financial assets.

Because funds are increasingly channelled into the purchase of existing financial assets rather than into economic investment, growth and even maintenance of the real economy is curtailed and impaired, which then requires debt financed consumption.

Under plutonomy's rule the financial sector's profit-seeking activities become focused primarily on the buying, selling, packaging and repackaging of either existing financial assets or new ones attached to existing real assets. Success at this pursuit and the creation of financial bubbles are interlinked. Leverage is used both to increase asset holdings and to inflate their price. The rising prices attract investors, especially pension funds, from outside the plutonomy's inner core which inflates prices still more until eventually bubbles burst. But bubbles burst because some people sell off at the top, leaving themselves with proportionately huge profits. They then wait for the bubble to deflate before buying back in with, if they wish, a much larger stake than before. For these people (And where other than The One Percent are they likely to me found?) it is the bursting of bubbles as much as their creation that makes them richer still.

5. Conclusion

The three and a half years of economic history since the bursting of the last bubble testify to the entrenched, unchallenged and still increasing power of the plutonamists. Unlike after the Crash of 29, nearly all of the government funds injected into the economy – and they have been of an historically unprecedented magnitude for peacetime – have gone **not** into the real economy, but instead into re-inflating the market-value of financial assets, owned in the main by The One Percent. The result was entirely predictable. The pair of the charts for the United States below sum up the radically different fates of the two dimensions of the economy and of their two corresponding groups of citizens.

Exhibit 9: Civilian Employment-Population Ratio – United States 2000 – 2012

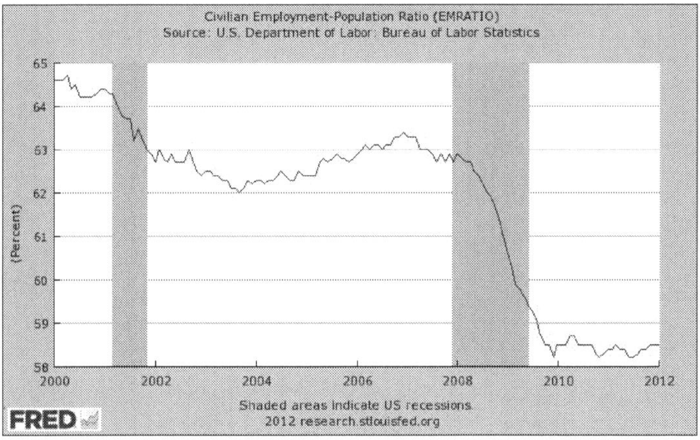

Exhibit 10: Dow Jones 2000–2008

Source: http://www.digitallook.com/-security.cgi?csi=50096&username=&ac=

The political-economic structure that created the current global crisis, and also the DotCom bubble and crash that preceded it, is unlikely to change any time soon. True, there is in the United States, and to a lesser extent in the UK, much public anger regarding the recent collapse and its consequences. But until very recently there was neither a constructive and realistic narrative nor an organizational vehicle through which to harness that public anger. Instead the Tea Party movement was cleverly funded by plotonomists as a means of channelling public anger in a way that strengthens the political base of plutonomy and promises to further accentuate the upward redistribution of income. Likewise the recent successful selling of Austerity.

More significant in the longer run is that any inhibitions that The One Percent may have had about creating bubbles should now be greatly reduced. The largest financial institutions, the ones most involved in creating bubbles, are now confident, whereas they were not a few years ago, that if they should fail to liquidate their holdings before the next bubble bursts, they will be bailed out at taxpayers' expense. Their executives also know that they will not be prosecuted for their frauds and that their billions of pounds of bonuses will continue to be paid.

For pro-democracy people the recent emergence of the Occupy or 99 Percent Movement is both a positive step and the sort of thing that the Citigroup reports cite as the ultimate danger to continued plutonomy rule. But that movement still exists only at the margins. It is much too early to tell if it will grow to have, directly or indirectly, an influence at the polls, nor even through what channels such influence might be realized. Furthermore there is not yet at the public level a narrative that identifies and focuses on the relevant political-economic structures, and explains how their policies have created and will in the future create financial bubbles which end with global crises and further upward redistributions of income. In short, regarding the political economy of today's world, in key countries ignorance prevails.

Index

45583332R00096

Printed in Poland
by Amazon Fulfillment
Poland Sp. z o.o., Wrocław